LIKE, FOLLOW, SHARE

LIKE, FOLLOW, SHARE

AWESOME, ACTIONABLE SOCIAL MEDIA MARKETING TO MAXIMIZE YOUR ONLINE POTENTIAL

SUSE BARNES

TYCHO
PRESS

CONTENTS

INTRODUCTION

The social media revolution has ended. It is now the new normal. The emergence and continuously increasing ubiquity of social media has been a revolution whose impact on our lifestyles many liken to the industrial revolution of the 19th century or, more commonly, the invention of the printing press. Even if these comparisons may be somewhat exaggerated, they are not ludicrous. The spread of social media has created new ways for people to communicate and interact with each other, and not just in the personal sphere, but with businesses as well. Just note how often you see Facebook and Twitter icons on TV ads, news shows, in magazines, on food packaging, not to mention on websites and blogs.

Our access to information and worldwide communication has changed more in the past few years than perhaps during any other time in human history. In 2010, then Google CEO Eric Schmidt said: "we create as much information in two days now as we did from the dawn of man through 2003." Where does most of that information come from? A lot of it is user-generated content. For example: 300 hours of video are uploaded to YouTube every minute, and every day people watch hundreds of millions of hours on YouTube and generate billions of views (www.youtube.com/yt/press/statistics.html).

It is now easier and faster than ever before to communicate directly with people and companies all over the world, and for free at that. Social media has transformed the way people define their own needs and wants, learn about products and services, become fans, shop, compare, negotiate, and in all other ways do business online. The social media environment on the Internet is so expansive and complicated that we will here prefer to call it the "social media universe." And we know this much for sure: it is starkly different from the traditional marketing universe of popup or banner ads, TV ads, newspaper ads, or billboards. While individually we are still just specks of dust in this vast universe, collectively as fans and followers we can have a significant influence on the world of commerce and society as a whole.

The most fundamental feature that differentiates social media is that the old world of advertising was a "push," essentially a one-way interaction where companies produced advertising, stuck it in front of a viewer, and hoped the viewer would be convinced to buy something. This is the very nature of broadcast communication. Products were mass-marketed; advertisements were aimed at an amorphous general public, or, at best, at certain vaguely defined age or gender groups. Companies rarely heard from their customers or members of the public, unless they undertook market research or some kind of survey or poll. Customer service was a department in itself. However, in the social media universe, that old monologue from company to customer has been replaced by a two-way interaction, an actual dialogue between companies and their customers. It's a universe where companies receive a previously unimaginable amount of input, feedback, questions, and complaints from their customers. The funnel has been reversed. It is no longer acceptable for companies to just tout their virtues and broadcast how great they are to consumers. Now consumers have a voice, and people are listening to each other more than to staid broadcast messages from businesses. Social media is a customer service channel, a public relations arena, an advertising platform, and an excellent means for building brand awareness and increasing brand loyalty. Now companies can learn, in real time, exactly what their customers want and expect. Not only that, but customers are free to talk among themselves as well, comparing prices, sharing recommendations and experiences—in essence, forming public opinion across social media networks. Now your customers define your brand.

"Goodbye Broadcast. Hello Conversation."
—Shel Israel (2009) *Twitterville: How Businesses Can Thrive in the New Global Neighborhoods.*

This is the new universe your business must navigate if you want to be successful in 2015 and beyond. However, it is a rapidly expanding and ever changing universe: The laws of nature in the social media universe are still being researched, and indeed still being created. Its vast spaces are expanding even as they are being charted and explored. The light of its fading stars (like MySpace) still guides us, even if only negatively, by pushing us in multiple directions and forcing us to keep up with the rocket speed of change.

The first and foundational law of nature of the social media universe is the law of interaction. Also known as engagement, interaction is evidence of interest. Take any basic definition of the word "social" and you'll find something along these lines: "friendly companionship or relations," "living or disposed to live in a community rather than in isolation," and "friendly, gregarious." Social media, by definition, is all about the bonds, conversations, and relationships that happen between and among people. Social media is fundamentally about participating in a community, and that is what has made it so successful. The various social media platforms all provide a means of connecting and interacting, whether one-to-one as individuals, in groups, or with other entities such as companies and governments. The reason why social media sites such as Facebook, Twitter, and LinkedIn have grown to become so enormous and so dominant is that they, each in its own way, address the deep-seated human need for interaction. People want to be seen and heard.

But keep in mind that it's not just people that interact; companies are expected to interact as well. That means your company has to have a social media presence, but it's not enough to just create a website or blog and let it sit there, passively existing. Your company has to actively contribute something to the conversation (we'll be discussing what to contribute in more detail later). And after you've said something, or made a contribution, you need to listen out for the response of the community. Members of the public will speak up to let you know if they approve, disagree, enjoy, or support what you have put forth. You will have to listen to their feedback and then reply—it's a never-ending cycle. It's a conversation. It's social media interaction. You are engaging with your audience. It's a dialog.

The second law of nature of the social media universe is the law of immediacy, specifically temporal immediacy, or as it is sometimes also called, "real time." Immediacy refers to "direct and instant involvement with something, giving rise to a sense of urgency or excitement," and that perfectly sums up the speed of life in the social media universe. Today's technology allows us to instantly access nearly any information we

THE CONVERSATION PRISM

Brought to you by
Brian Solis & JESS3

The Conversation Prism. *Source:* www.conversationprism.com[1]

could possibly wish to find, no matter how obscure or specific. Finding something happens as quickly as you can type it into your Google search bar, and even the most inaccessible content is rarely more than a few clicks away. This same sense of immediacy holds true with our contacts and networks; we can communicate with our colleagues, friends, and family on the other side of the world via text, email, a messaging app, or even live video via Skype or, for example, Google Hangouts, and they receive our message within seconds. Not only that, but we expect a reply within seconds as well. Having to wait one hour for something seems to be a positively glacial pace. On social media channels, content is being continuously created, posted, and updated. Many people check social media multiple times a day—or even multiple times an hour—to make sure that they haven't missed something, because all of the information rolls by so quickly. We often refer to social media information as a stream (particularly on Twitter) or a feed (as in Facebook's newsfeed). Things become "old" in a matter of not days, but hours or even minutes.

Each social network has its own half-life for each post. For example, when you post something on Facebook, it may be visible for up to 30 to 60 minutes in the various newsfeeds of your fans, (i.e., people who like your business). On Twitter, on the other hand, a tweet likely only has a half-life of 15 seconds to 15 minutes, because the feed is updating much more frequently, more people are posting in real-time, and people on Twitter have much bigger numbers in terms of followers than people on Facebook. I don't have specific data, because each social account serves a unique purpose and reaches a unique audience, but the point is that you should think of social media posts as similar to growing a garden or building a relationship. Both require regular and consistent nurturing. The different platforms, however, have different rules for how to engage with fans on each. Just as there are different rules for different modes of transport (driving a car, taking the train, flying a plane), there are differ-ent rules for getting places via different social channels. Know the rules and you'll reach your destination on time and at the price you expected to pay. Jump in trying to figure it out along the way, and you may find yourself reinventing a few wheels.

Due to this sense of immediacy, there are new expectations and a new etiquette in the social media universe. This applies to companies as well

Social Business: Not If, But When

BY DAVID ARMANO

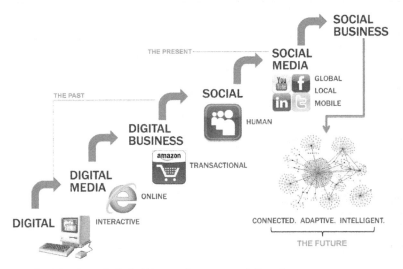

The Future of Social Business. *Credit:* David Armano. *Source:* www.sprinklr.com[2]

as people. If you respond or take another action too slowly, you risk being perceived as "not with it," perhaps disorganized or incompetent, or, even worse, as rude and uncaring. To function successfully you'll have to adapt to working at the speed of the Internet, or, more accurately, the speed of social. It's warp speed, but don't let that scare you! This is actually a rather positive development, which can certainly be used to your advantage. As we discussed at the beginning of this section, immediacy creates a sense of excitement, which you can use to great effect.

Social media platforms (and social media marketing) have truly revolutionized the way we do business, both globally and locally, and continue to do so. They provide opportunities and possibilities that would have been unimaginable just a few years ago. And they will only continue to evolve, surprising us all with coming developments. This is a great time to jump into social media, and if you can master *interaction, immediacy* and *responsiveness* you'll be well on your way to producing a successful social media marketing strategy.

PART

CHAPTER 1

YOU & YOUR WORK

Maybe you are entirely new to social media and don't yet know the difference between Twitter and Instagram. Maybe you find yourself thinking: What the heck is a "tweet" anyway? Or perhaps you have dabbled a bit in social media: You recently created a Facebook account (because everyone else seems to have one), which you rarely use, but could probably manage to navigate if you really had to. Perhaps you have a Facebook account purely for promoting your business and you don't use it for connecting with friends at all.

Maybe you're a bit beyond the beginner level; you've got a huge Facebook network, you post on Twitter regularly, and you've got a knockout Pinterest page. You're fairly active on your chosen networks, but that's personal use—how are you supposed to use social media for marketing? How can you use it to promote your company? Businesses using Snapchat as a marketing channel seems unfathomable to you.

Or, at the farther end of the spectrum, maybe you're pretty much an expert. You're social media savvy; perhaps you're even responsible for your company's social media marketing strategy, or for managing one of their pages. You're just not quite yet getting the results you want. You need to go deeper, learning best practices and ways to optimize your social media presence and really make it shine. You want to connect with your fans, boost engagement, and boost sales as well. In short, you need to take it to the next level. And you're starting to realize the kind of time and effort this might take.

Sidenote: In one of the first social media marketing classes I taught, I divided the class up into self-designated levels of social media expertise. I called these Advanced, Beginner, and Comfortable, for the simple use of ABC. It worked well, as students felt a sense of community with other students at a similar place in their learning timeline. We're not all in the same place in terms of experience, but we can all learn from each other. No one knows everything about social media, not even the experts, and this is particularly true for social media because it is an ever-changing industry. To succeed in social media you need to be constantly learning and updating your skills.

Whether you're a beginner or an expert, a freelancer or a CEO, you're reading this book because you know that social media is important. Indeed, your company cannot afford to ignore it; it is the world's preferred method of connecting, communicating, learning, discovering products and services, seeking reviews, networking, shopping, sharing.... You already know that your business is expected to have an online presence, but how should you proceed? You need to figure out which social media sites are most relevant to your company and how to use them effectively to reach your audience. You need to understand enough about the basics to make informed decisions and ask the right questions—questions such as: How much time should we devote to developing our social media pages? How will we know if they're successful? What results can we expect?

No matter what line of work you're in, or what kind of profile you ultimately end up building, there are a few key points that are true of social media in general. First of all, social media marketing is not free. In the early days, social media was hailed as a platform for "free" advertising. Of course it is free to join all of the major social networking sites, and free to post content, so you aren't likely to spend as much money as you might have with traditional advertising like a TV commercial, for example. But you will need to devote both time and money to achieve sustained growth. You may need to dedicate a full-time employee (or even a team or a whole department) to maintaining your social media pages. Creating quality content takes time, effort, and possibly a budget for equipment, supplies, or technology. Depending on how intensively you use social media, you'll need to allocate people and resources to stay current, respond to questions and complaints, monitor posts and mentions, and develop material.

Secondly, you cannot expect results from social media overnight. It's a marathon, not a sprint. Just as building a relationship in real life takes time, so does building a connection with your audience on social media. Even the best of pages and companies do not get thousands of instant followers and huge sales right away. Social media requires consistent, sustained work. You will be generating interest, referrals, word-of-mouth buzz, gradually building your reputation, and earning the trust and loyalty of your followers one by one. In the long term, this will be a huge asset to your company. Just don't give up after Week One!

Finally, social media will never be able to make up for a bad product or weak organization. In fact, social media will actually reveal any deficiencies your company may have with brutal quickness, in a way that traditional advertising never would have done. Your customers will quickly let you— and everyone else—know about rude employees, faulty products, or other failures. Social media is a giant platform for word-of-mouth information, and stories spread quickly. Fortunately, there are ways you can pro- actively deal with negative comments (see chapter 9), and the feedback can actually strengthen your company if you are willing to act on it.

You want to do the best for your company. If you're a beginner, this book should get you solidly on the path to social media competence by providing an overview, acquainting you with general principles, and explaining the basics. If you're already proficient in social media, this book should help you improve your strategy with plenty of new and cre- ative suggestions, examples, and technical tips for optimizing your pages.

To begin with, you'll learn to assess which social networks will work best for you. We will cover the primary uses of various social networking sites and which kinds of industries are best suited to each one. We'll discuss who uses them and how they function in a general sense. You'll also learn about defining your goals. What are realistic expectations for social media, and how can you reach them? That includes using metrics and analytic tools to help you track your progress. You'll want to perform an audit where you will assess the current state of your social media plan and figure out what is missing. How are your customers responding to you, and what can you do better? It's important to identify what is working for you as well as areas where improvement is needed. You'll get recommendations for producing high-quality content, humanizing your brand, building relationships, optimizing engagement, and rewarding fan loyalty. Ready? Let's do it!

CHAPTER 2

BRANDING YOURSELF

Your brand is what identifies your company and differentiates your product or service from others. Like your face, it's a way people recognize you. The term "branding" and the practice it names originated with livestock branding. Farm animals were given a distinguishing mark via a brand being burned into their skin so that they wouldn't get mixed up with neighbors' or competitors' livestock. For business and your career, it is important to brand your company and/or your own individual self with something unique that will stick in the minds of your customers and potential customers. Branding often involves a logo or symbol, which people remember over time and associate with you, but it may also be a feeling. What we want as business owners, job seekers, or even singles looking for a date is to be thought of as worthy, respectable, attractive, and valued.

Your brand is what identifies you. "Brand name" is usually juxtaposed with "generic": a generic brand is the subpar knockoff of the original or better-known brand. Having a brand identity makes you stand out in the crowd as offering something distinctive: the best, or coolest, or edgiest, or cheapest, or safest, (and so on), product in your area. Your brand identity encompasses and should evoke your reputation, your character, your characteristic or flagship items, your history, and other narratives you use to distinguish yourself. If you are successful in creating a brand, you create an association in people's minds such that whenever they see your brand or hear its name, they think of something unique. This brand association may encompass a word or phrase, a symbol, logo, or other characteristic image, a color pattern, a sound bite like Wendy's "Where's the beef?," or even your product's packaging, as in Apple's satisfyingly sleek minimalist packaging—all of which can directly bring forth in the mind of your customers and potential customers all sorts of (hopefully positive) associations. People will know what to expect. They will feel safe in the decision they make to engage with (or avoid, as the case may be) your offering. Take for example the Nike swoosh. This symbol is so etched into our collective social consciousness that there are very few people who will not know what the symbol represents. And what does it represent? What is the association that comes to mind when you see the swoosh? Is it running shoes, soccer, fitness apparel, advancement in athletic shoe design, or Michael Jordan? And, regardless of which of these springs to mind, you will likely also remember the tagline "Just Do It," which conveys a feeling of strength, endurance, and courage.

Think of the bell logo that Taco Bell uses. If you see that on a hot sauce bottle being sold in the supermarket, your mind immediately conjures up your experiences and associations with Taco Bell and affixes them to the bottle of hot sauce. Perhaps you like Taco Bell, but have always found the miniscule salsa packets they give out ridiculous. If that's the case, the brand recognition and that particular experience can combine to make you see the full bottle of Taco Bell hot sauce as exactly what you need for the next time you bring Taco Bell home.

Think about big brands and smaller brands that you prefer, and think about why they are unique and memorable to you. What makes you buy your favorite brands over and over? Are you loyal to some brands and not at all to others? Do you know why? Chances are you probably have strong feelings about why you use one brand over another, and these reasons make up the brand's equity and your brand loyalty.

So how do you create a brand identity in your social media marketing? Step one is to make sure you have a distinctive name for your enterprise, one that will not be lost in a flood of similar search results. There was once a punk band who gave themselves the name "Sexvid." It is literally impossible to find any of their content online, because an Internet search of that term brings up legions of pornography, but not punk music. So in picking a name, or logo, or motto for your enterprise, you not only need to think of the characteristic offer and identity you are making for yourself, you also need to pick a distinctive search term. Avoid using special characters like &, %, or # in your name, because these are not so easily dealt with by most search engines or online channels.

The second consideration is content. In the social media world, the identity of your brand will be associated with the content you provide. Catchy, stimulating, and informative content will motivate people to return to your page, share it with their friends, subscribe to your posts, and so on. Provide content that is not only directly related to your product or service, but also indirectly related; that way you can emphasize the relevance or broader interest of what you are doing, and find more ways to keep people interested. For example, if you manufacture headphones, you can post or link to content related to new music, controversies regarding the consolidation of streaming music services, tutorials about the difference between MP3, AIFF, and FLAC files, and so on. You want to set up a place where people will have many reasons to visit. That will establish your brand identity as dynamic, informative, and trustworthy.

Think of the content (blog posts, articles, social posts, videos, photos, and sites) that you enjoy reading and engaging with. Now think of how you can provide content in your industry that offers the same kind of value as the content you personally enjoy.

In social media, being straightforward and direct usually produces better rapport with your viewers and customers than being superficially flashy and loud. For one thing, flashy graphics and audio may cause some people's devices to hiccup. For another, the social media environment is one that should encourage a multidimensional conversation between you and your customers, as well as among your customers themselves. Being flashy and "knock 'em over the head" is a mode of establishing identity that is oriented by the paradigm of static media like billboards or magazine adds. Those kinds of engagements are one-way. Remember: "Goodbye broadcast. Hello Conversation." The most distinctive feature of social media is the immediacy of interactions it enables: People value the interactive dimension of social media, and they want something they can make a meaningful contribution to, or learn something of value from. No one likes to talk in a vacuum. Provide customers and potential customers with a forum on which to engage other users/viewers/potential and actual customers, and you are building a community around your brand. People want to be seen and heard. They want to feel like they are part of your community and that they are valued.

In conclusion, branding comes down to defining an identity for your company, and then being true to that identity in the way you conduct business and express yourself via social media. Your reputation as a company will be strongly associated with your brand. First of all, you should consider your identity: What is it that makes your company different? Think of something you can say about your company that starts with "Only we …" What are your strengths as a company? And what is it that you will promise and deliver to your customers? What are your goals? What do you want the public to think about your company? What image do you hope to project? Are you a humorous company? Serious? Outrageous? Nerdy? Next, consider your audience and communication style. Depending on your company personality, and who you are speaking with, you'll need to select the appropriate language, tone, and social media platform. This is the "voice" of your brand. Finally, refine and personalize your image to align it with the identity and personality

Chocolate for Breakfast Owner Sue Ann Gleason. *Source:* www.chocolateforbreakfast.com[3]

of your company. This may include visual images, such as logos, color palettes, fonts, photos, and so on. We'll be discussing your online persona (or representation of your brand) further in the next chapter.

It's often easy to think that social media is a platform for you to show off, brag, or share all your wonderful capabilities with the world. But remember, social media is not about "me." That is, it is not about you as a person or you as a company. Social media is a dialogue, a means to conversation and membership in one or more communities. The companies that understand this are the ones succeeding in social media.

Take, for example, Chocolate for Breakfast. Sue Ann Gleason is a nutritionist with an acute understanding of her audience. She built a website and Facebook page called Chocolate for Breakfast to appeal

Sample post from Chocolate for Breakfast—Jan 17, 2015. *Source:* www.facebook.com[4]

to people who love chocolate, knowing full well that most of them are concerned about their diet and nutrition. Her tagline is "Where pleasure meets permission." The Facebook page is updated regularly with delicious pictures of chocolate, and Sue is extremely responsive to comments from fans. She doesn't make people feel guilty about loving chocolate, and instead offers ways for people who love chocolate to connect over their common interest and, indeed, passion. For many of her 28,047 fans, Sue Ann symbolizes that you can have your chocolate and eat it too. She provides nutrition consultation, sells recipe books, and, since she has done so well with her Chocolate for Breakfast business in social media, she is now also a social media marketing consultant. Here's someone who has successfully built her online persona and is reaping the rewards admirably.

CHAPTER 3

CREATING AN ONLINE PERSONA

A persona is a character. The root word "persona" in Latin actually means "mask," and so a persona also refers to your public or outward face (as sometimes distinct from your inward face, what lies underneath the mask). Your persona is the character you present to others, and, especially on social media, it is always your audience who has the final say about the value of the features of this character. Constructing a persona involves imagining yourself from the outside, from the perspective of others: How do you want to be seen by others? Your character needs to be responsive to the concerns of your audience. In other words, your persona needs to have a virtuous character. You might think it sounds weird to say that you need to create a mask or character for your enterprise online, but this is actually no different from what people normally do in their everyday lives. I put on one mask to show when I'm home visiting my family, another when I am out with my friends, and another when I am in a professional setting. You are who you are in the listening. That is to say, people who hear you and see you reflect back your image to you. Others around you partly define your persona. Social media marketing is an extension of the way you "market" yourself to other people in social situations. Just as in the everyday life of a real flesh-and-blood person, the task of creating a trustable and likeable persona for a business brings up a whole nest of thorny issues: how you look, what you want to achieve (goals), and your overall attitude (including honesty, authenticity, originality, and transparency). This chapter covers each of these areas for you.

3.1 LOOKS

The first thing we notice on another person is (usually) their looks, whether it is the look of their face, or the look of their outfit or hairstyle, or how their clothes fall on their body, and so on. Looks are absolutely crucial for taking charge of first impressions and creating instantaneous memories that may be triggered again and built upon later. Since everything in social media happens so fast—most people will only very briefly pass their eyes over your content, or maybe only catch it out of the corner of their eye while they are focusing on something else—you need to grab the attention of the customer so that they linger on a bit longer or do a double take.

How to best catch someone's attention will differ by social platform (blog, Instagram, Facebook, etc.), but we can make a few generalizations. First of all, since social media interactions are a digital mutation of everyday interactions between flesh-and-blood human beings, your look should be, broadly speaking, human, which is also to say humane. Studies have shown that images of smiling human beings looking outward and making eye contact with the viewer are more successful at creating a positive feeling and generating a tendency to look at the image longer. Try smiling at a few people and count how many times they don't smile back. Chances are that they will all return your smile. Thanks to mirror neurons, seeing another person smile or laugh triggers our brain to fire in the same regions that would be firing if we ourselves were smiling and laughing; it may even literally make us smile or laugh ourselves, thereby further cementing, on a primal biological level, a positive association with your brand. Of course the same thing is true of images of people scowling, screaming, or suffering, so avoid those images.

The general lesson is to humanize your brand and turn it into "someone" that people on social media will want to interact with. Create a look that will cater to your target audience's persona—one that they will feel comfortable and happy to be interacting with (like), one that will inspire them to show your content to others (share), one they want to keep looking at when no one else is watching (follow).

Your look is particularly important for visual learners. Humans can be divided into three types of learners and thus consumers of information:

visual, auditory, and kinesthetic. In addition to having a look, you need to cultivate a particular "voice" in the text you present and in the way you respond to comments. As with the look, the appropriate style of your voice will depend on what kind of customers you are trying to reach and appeal to. Do you keep it formal and devoid of Internet abbreviations (e.g., "ur" for "your," "2" for "to" or "too")? Do you use emoticons? What about exclamation points? Straightforward text can feel deadened compared to living spoken language, so people often resort to adding extra punctuation in order to convey emphasis and emotion. Your "voice" appeals to the auditory learner in us as well as the kinesthetic, because what you say in words often affects how the recipients feel. Maya Angelou said, "I've learned that people will forget what you said, people will forget what you did, but people will never forget how you made them feel."

Remember that tone is extremely difficult to convey in text on the web—your sarcasm or irony may be taken totally seriously, since the usual facial expressions and tonal variations that we can rely on in everyday interactions are absent there. This is part of the reason for the increasing popularity of emoticons. The "eye-winking" can make it more acceptable for you to say something quirky and funny that can help you gain trust and good feelings from your customers. Without the "eye winking" emoticon, though, a quirky statement may be very easily misinterpreted. For example, "That chocolate cake was wicked! ☺" conveys a very different meaning from "That chocolate cake was wicked! ☹"

3.2 GOALS

Your online persona has to feel like a real person to your audience. Whenever a person does something, you can ask them "Why did you do that?" Their response will specify the reasons for their action and what goals they were trying to accomplish. If a person acts randomly, makes plans and then breaks them, doesn't answer your calls, and engages in activities that contradict each other or don't add up to any coherent plan, you will not want to interact with that person. You wouldn't trust any person like that, and therefore you probably wouldn't want to buy anything from them.

The activities of your online persona need to be guided by goals.

The overall point of a social media presence is to build and sustain relationships with your customers, which will serve the overall business goal of increasing revenue. This means that one guiding general goal of your online persona needs to be tending to the customers' needs and concerns. Take care of your customer, and the profit will take care of itself. Build relationships first and make money later.

The more specific goals of your online persona will vary depending on the particular product, service, or offer you are putting forward. Perhaps your goal is to recruit new followers, raise awareness of your brand, tell everyone about a cool new product, boost sales, increase customer loyalty, or reward long-time fans. It's a good idea to pick one realistic goal at a time and focus on that. For example, you might start with a goal such as "I want to increase online sales by 20% in the next quarter." This is an example of a SMART goal. SMART stands for Specific, Measurable, Attainable, Realistic, and Time-bound. Once you have a goal you can start building a strategy. Then, when you implement your strategy, you will use social media analytics tools and other metrics to track your progress towards your goal.

SMART Goal Setting. *Source:* www.shutterstockphoto.com[5]

3.3 ATTITUDE: HONESTY, AUTHENTICITY, ORIGINALITY, TRANSPARENCY

The final and most important consideration to take into account when cultivating your online persona is to convey a trustworthy and likeable overall attitude. The main virtues of such an attitude are honesty, authenticity, originality, and transparency. These are virtues we all expect from our good friends. And now, thanks to the immediacy and potentially viral publicity of content on social media, these virtues are a necessity for any social media marketing strategy.

The social media marketer is in charge of the public projection of honesty, authenticity, originality, and transparency. There needs to be tight coordination between what is projected by your online persona and the actions that are executed within your company.

HONESTY

The first key to trust is honesty. People are much more likely to develop loyalty to a brand they trust. Luckily, honesty is pretty simple to cultivate. Don't lie. Do not make offers you will not or cannot keep. Try not to say things just because people want to hear them. Try to be consistent in the way your treat your customers. People are good at finding out information on the Internet and from each other, and they won't hesitate to broadcast it to the world if they sense that you are being dishonest with them. Information flows in a way that will be beyond your control,

 Christina Marie @CKMarie23 · Feb 16
Snow sucks. So did my drive home from the airport. I need my bed. Wasn't planning on being home at 3am. Thanks @SouthwestAir #welcomehome

12:53 AM · 16 Feb 2015 · Details

Southwest Airlines @SouthwestAir · Feb 16
@CKMarie23 We're glad to see you are safe! Our apologies for the delay, we know they're frustrating and we appreciate your patience. ^AC

@SouthWestAir showing that they are listening and offering an apology. *Source:* Twitter Stream for @ckMarie23[6]

so don't fool yourself into thinking you can cover your tracks for very long if you are being dishonest. Remember that since social media interactions are not one-way, they are not like an ad in a newspaper or on a billboard, and so customers (actual and potential) always have the ability to respond to your statements and activities. You can never shut down a conversation by dodging a question or offering a partial answer or a half-truth. Users have come to feel empowered by the ability to say anything they want to a potentially limitless audience, and you have to take that power seriously.

AUTHENTICITY

People can smell inauthenticity a mile off, and it smells bad. What is inauthenticity? It is when you are showing up as someone who just follows a predefined script; someone who doesn't actually express themselves or put their real self on the line in a situation, or in response to someone else's concerns. You can feel that someone is being inauthentic when you sense they are just saying things to you that they think you want to hear, or when they treat you as just the bearer of a general demographic category (e.g., a woman, a teenager, an old person) rather than as a unique individual, or when they are saying things that are not grounded in their actual values and commitments, but just fit what they seem to think is most advantageous in this situation. You cannot trust someone who comes off as inauthentic. You cannot take them seriously, and you probably would not give them your money.

Authenticity, on the other hand, is intrinsically attractive to other people. Authenticity is when there is no mismatch between the outward behavior and the inward motivations. We say someone is authentic when they truly express themselves in the situation, rather than catering to an audience in some kind of performance. Hence, authenticity is also about treating people as the individuals they are—hearing their voice, taking their concerns seriously—rather than as statistics or bearers of a label or as anonymous and replaceable placeholders. We trust people who are authentic, and we want to be around them and continue to interact with them, because they help us feel valued for who we are too.

That being said, how in the world can an online persona be authentic? After all, there might be several people behind the scenes creating the online persona and interacting with other social media users. On the face of it, authenticity doesn't look like something a mere persona can have. Does an online persona have any stable or unified values or commitments or personality characteristics that it can either live up to in its behavior or fail to live up to? Absolutely. Part of your persona is to have a character with particular personality traits, values, and commitments, and these always need to guide the interactions of your online persona (no matter which particular employee is pressing the actual buttons). You need to interact with your customers in such a way that they feel that you are responding directly to them, person-to-person, not machine or actor to person.

How do you show you are an authentic brand on social media? Make it your project to be real and to be human. Be real: Using the framework of your company's core values and desired voice, respond directly to customers who comment and mention you in their comments. Don't rely on fake-sounding canned, generic responses. Being authentic also means owning up to and taking responsibility for mistakes. Speaking of mistakes, don't be afraid to make mistakes (mistaken facts, names, spellings, etc.) and then correct them. This helps show that there is a person behind the persona and not just an automated system treating the customers as interchangeable specimens.

For example, four years ago, the odd tweet below was posted by the American Red Cross.

American Red Cross
@RedCross

Ryan found two more 4 bottle packs of Dogfish Head's Midas Touch beer.... when we drink we do it right #gettngslizzerd

HootSuite · 2/15/11 11:24 PM

Tweet posted by the American Red Cross. *Source:* www.mashable.com[7]

Confused? You should be. A Red Cross employee inadvertently posted a tweet on Twitter client Hootsuite using their work Twitter account (rather than their personal account) while they were obviously at a party.

@riaglo
Gloria Huang

Rogue tweet frm @RedCross due to my inability to use hootsuite... I wasn't actually #gettingslizzard but just excited! #nowembarassing

4 hours ago via HootSuite ☆ Favorite ↻ Retweet ↩ Reply

Tweet by Red Cross employee admitting her mistake.
Source: www.mashable.com[8]

Gloria Huang confessed to the mistake on her own personal account admitting embarrassment, and then @RedCross responded with the tongue-in-cheek response below. This is an excellent way of defusing a challenging situation. Not only did @RedCross admit their mistake, they also humanized the situation and gave people following their Twitter stream a little reason to laugh as well. The American Red Cross actually got quite a bit of buzz around this at the time, because it is a great example of responsive crisis management. It is better to admit the mistake than to try to hide it, and this is especially true on social media.

We've deleted the rogue tweet but rest assured the Red Cross is sober and we've confiscated the keys.

about 11 hours ago via ÜberTwitter
Retweeted by 86 people

RedCross
American Red Cross

Swift crisis response by American Red Cross earned them a lot of social media mentions. *Source:* www.mashable.com[9]

Even though the Red Cross deleted the tweet, many people took screenshots of it to blog about, because it is a great example for other companies to learn from, and it made for a good little story.

In this regard, that is, in showing that there is a real person behind the persona (which will help reinforce the authenticity effect), it is a good idea to sometimes post behind-the-scenes photographs of the social media team at work. Also, have each person on the social media team who may be authoring posts under the company name initial their posts with their own initials. @HiltonSuggests does this on Twitter to identify each concierge associate who is responding to questions posted on Twitter about cities in which there are Hilton hotels. Each tweet is a response to a person's question posted on Twitter, and each response contains the initials of the responder at the end of the response with a caret preceding the initials (e.g., ^MLA).

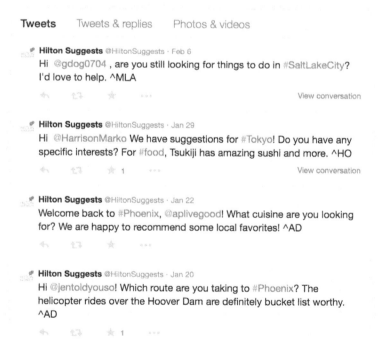

Tweets   Tweets & replies   Photos & videos

Hilton Suggests @HiltonSuggests · Feb 6
Hi @gdog0704 , are you still looking for things to do in #SaltLakeCity? I'd love to help. ^MLA

View conversation

Hilton Suggests @HiltonSuggests · Jan 29
Hi @HarrisonMarko We have suggestions for #Tokyo! Do you have any specific interests? For #food, Tsukiji has amazing sushi and more. ^HO

1   View conversation

Hilton Suggests @HiltonSuggests · Jan 22
Welcome back to #Phoenix, @aplivegood! What cuisine are you looking for? We are happy to recommend some local favorites! ^AD

Hilton Suggests @HiltonSuggests · Jan 20
Hi @jentoldyouso! Which route are you taking to #Phoenix? The helicopter rides over the Hoover Dam are definitely bucket list worthy. ^AD

1

@HiltonSuggests Twitter stream shows that they are listening for questions relating to a particular city and then answering each question as best they can. Their strategy is to be helpful. *Source:* www.twitter.com[10]

This way you are being forthright about there being a whole team of people producing these responses, rather than pretending to be some mysterious unified "voice" of the company. After all, all of your customers already know that there has to be someone authoring the messages (that is, assuming the messages are not automated, an impression you never want to give), so you should directly own up to that and be authentic with your audience.

ORIGINALITY

Being original is perhaps both the easiest and the most difficult virtue to cultivate for your persona's character. To be original means to originate your own content and to project a distinctive and memorable presence via a social media persona. You want to offer something what will encourage your customers to become fans and then take it upon themselves to share your content, thus creating organic word of mouth in your customers' communities. The easy part is that there is just one constraint on being original: that you are not copying other companies. The hard part is that there is just one constraint on being original: Don't copy what others are doing. How exactly are you supposed to come up with something that isn't being done by other companies? In a nutshell: creative experimentation. Social media happens at such a fast pace that you can experiment with many different approaches, as well as variations on, or reversals of, what others have done.

@HiltonSuggests is one example. Their strategy is just to be helpful. Each trained concierge member searches for questions posted on Twitter regarding their city, and responds with valuable answers. The people asking the questions aren't even necessarily staying at the Hilton in that city, but since the person asking the question received a customized and highly valuable answer to their question, that person is much more likely to consider staying at a Hilton in the future. Hilton is effectively making a friend every time they answer a question, and people are posting questions when traveling away from home quite frequently.

Another good example is Oreo, who responded with "Real-Time Relevancy" during Super Bowl 2013 when there was a power failure at the game, with the posts below.

Oreo's famous tweet when the power went out at the Super Bowl in 2013. *Source:* www.imediaconnection.com[11]

"Real-Time Relevancy" is a term coined by Jay Baer in his 2013 book *Youtility: Why Smart Marketing Is about Help not Hype.* This kind of real-time responsiveness has evolved into big companies having war rooms or teams of social media managers at the ready during major events, to be able to respond to emerging situations with great immediacy.

To be original is to be memorable. So, rather than posting a picture of your product to your Instagram feed, for example, produce images of your product in unexpected contexts, or being put to unexpected uses. Figure out different ways to use current events as a way of showcasing your offerings, like Oreo does. They always have a campaign tailored to each holiday or big event. For example, for Valentine's Day they have made a series of short animated videos promoting their new red velvet Oreo product, and they have even built a whole site where you can explore all the different fun things they have done with social media so far (see www.oreoplay.com). You may also want to offer variations on

Science Channel ✔
February 12 · 🌐

Here's our version of #TBT. We bring you the kid who duct-taped himself to the ceiling from a previous episode of Outrageous Acts of Science.

It just has to be re-seen. Let us know if you agree. >> http://bit.ly/1vGC0VN

Hanging Out With Duct–Tape

Jason is spending his Saturday night being duct-taped to the ceiling. The question is, how does the duct-tape hold his 175 lbs.? It's all about van der Waals Forces.

SCIENCECHANNEL.COM

#TBT or Throw Back Thursday Facebook post from the Science Channel. *Source:* www.facebook.com[12]

#TBT, which means Throw Back Thursday, or do something like San Francisco's Pier 39 did on Facebook by showing photos that have been shared by real people visiting the pier. There is no shortage of ideas, and it's so easy to test them on social media that the best thing to do is experiment and keep refining based on what works best.

Most importantly: *Have fun*—this will be contagious and rub off on your customers, who will then be more likely to share your content or to bring it up in conversation with friends and family.

PIER 39
February 4 ·

We never get tired of this view.

Photo credit: forpriyank

Like · Comment · Share · 👍 953 💬 12 ↪ 47

PIER 39 credits visitors who have shared their pictures of PIER 39. *Source:* www.facebook.com[13]

TRANSPARENCY

What is fascinating about social media is the immediacy with which things happen there. This fact, that people communicate instantly and directly with each other, whether you intervene or not, means that you are bound to have a hard time covering up your mistakes, oversights, and failures. The best thing to do if they occur is own up to them right away and publicly. If you don't know the answer to a question or concern, don't pretend like you do. Go ahead and say you need some time to figure things out, and promise to get back to them within a day over a private message. People have grown to expect instantaneous responses, so do not let complaints or questions linger too long unaddressed on any of your pages or comments sections. The Internet has made us all impatient. Just think of how often you check your email everyday or even every hour! Next, when you learn about what may have gone wrong in the customer's transaction, offer them a public explanation (or a private one if that is more appropriate). This will impress them, because they will feel like they are being treated like a real person by a real person, which is crucial for building relationships and sustaining engagement. Having said that, when you are not playing defense you should feel free to inject a little bit of creative opacity into your social media posts. Mystery is an essential ingredient to seduction. You want to lure people back. So, be transparent in cases where your trustworthiness and accountability are on the line, and yet feel free to be a little flirtatious and mysterious sometimes as well, as long as it's all in line with the persona you are projecting.

CHAPTER 4

DEFINING YOUR AUDIENCE

4.1 INTRODUCTION: WHO IS YOUR TARGET AUDIENCE?

In my classes I like to use something that I learned from my colleague Avery Horzewski, which is the motto "A is for Audience." If you know whom you are talking with, you can craft your message so that they will be most receptive to it and want to share it everywhere. In order for this to work, you need a characterization of those people who will potentially buy your product or service (as well as those who already are buying it). There are several questions you'll want to ask or know the answers to. Think about this like trying to find a potential mate. You'll want to know as much as possible about the person you want to date, so that you can ask them for what you want in a way that they will be most likely to respond positively. Questions about your target audience may include: What are their concerns and values? What values do they share with you or your business? What benefits are they looking for? What do they like? Who are their friends? Where do they live (in the city, suburbs, or countryside)? What is their age, income, gender, ethnicity, relationship status, and sexual orientation? Are they politically conservative or liberal? Do they have a lot of siblings? What are their dietary preferences, hobbies, and passions?

Knowing the answers to all of these questions will help you tailor your content appropriately. For example, if your target audience is college guys in their early 20s, you may not want to include pictures of babies frolicking with cute puppies in your imagery. You want to reach people who will listen and feel like you actually understand and know them. You don't want to broadcast a message, but rather start a conversation. You want to engage them, and inspire them to keep engaging with you.

Just as you can't be everything to all people, you can't be in every conversation at once with the same voice. If you are targeting multiple demographics with divergent concerns and characteristics, create distinct content for each group, and target them specifically. They may well be frequenting different kinds of social media sites. Find out where your target audiences are hanging out online, and go there to deliver the content that you have specifically curated for them. Fish where the fish are. (A good free tool to find out where they are is www.socialmention.com. We'll talk more about this in Part Two.)

If you already have a following on social media, do your own research and ask them what they find valuable in your product or service; find out what their concerns and commitments are, and do more to engage them in those areas too. Social media offers an opportunity for you to listen and understand both your target audience and your existing customers.

4.2 BROWSER VS. CUSTOMER VS. FOLLOWER

As you are well aware, there are a lot of people on the Internet, and that number is growing at a phenomenal rate daily. All of these people are all at different stages of the buying cycle relative to your business. Some people are unaware of your offerings, others are just looking or browsing, some are already customers, and still others are your "brand ambassadors." It is a good idea to know in advance a few distinctions regarding different kinds of viewers of your content. This way you may be able to influence them into becoming a consistent customer, and you will be able to specifically target the different kinds of viewers of your content in ways that are more likely to convert them to being loyal fans and even advocates for your brand.

Since the social media universe is always a two-way-conversation universe, you need to build up your presence in it by anticipating what your viewers want to see and what they may be interested in talking about.

We will define **a browser** as someone who will happen upon your site or content by random browsing or some other contingency (recommendation from a friend or "friend," a tweet or retweet, etc.). Imagine the following scenario: A browser was not looking for you but nevertheless found you, and decides on the basis of your seductive and informational online presence to take a chance on your product or service. In order to attract browsers to be more interested in your content, you need to use certain incentives: These could include bargains, discounts, referrals, catchy or uniquely informative content, humor, or just something so completely unique that it makes them stop to look further. Your goal is to attract the browsers and make them stay. At this point the browser is a potential customer.

A customer is someone who has made a purchase from your company; someone who has come to know and trust your brand; someone who returns to and shares your online content; someone who feels heard and connected with your online persona. Customers develop loyalty, and they can even become what are called "brand ambassadors." Brand ambassadors or brand advocates are people who bring your message (product or service) to the rest of the world. They are more than happy to share thoughts and information about your product without you even asking them to. Think about diehard Apple fans who jump in the discussion whenever there are any negative comments about Apple, countering them with lots of positive comments and even ways to solve the unhappy person's product issues.

The goal of any enterprise is to produce customers, because customers ultimately mean profit. In the social media universe, though, you want to produce customers who are also followers, in other words, customer-followers.

A follower is a unique denizen of the social media universe. Followers are often "likes" on Facebook (i.e., people who like your page). They are called followers on Twitter, Instagram, Pinterest, and most other social networks, but on Facebook they are referred to as likes. Followers fall on a scale from curious browsers (could-be buyers) to serious diehard-fans (customer-followers) who are anxious to eat up every update. You need to guide your followers, but don't lead them. They need to feel that they are a partner in the transaction, because social media is interactive and people want to feel empowered. Many followers stay with you because of inertia, because, for some funny psychological reason, even for someone who is no longer interested in your content, pressing the "unfollow" button seems harder than scrolling down to the next thing. These inertial followers present an opportunity for you: You can turn them into potential buyers or customers. As for non-inertial followers, you will need to keep engaging with them so they don't get bored and follow someone else. Post something at least once a day on Facebook and possibly more frequently on other channels; otherwise, given the short attention span that the social media universe imposes on us, you may be forgotten or neglected. That being said, virtue is a golden mean between excess and deficiency, and if you post too many things (especially too many irrelevant things), you can easily annoy your followers and lose them. Followers can be flakey or they can be committed. Followers are only valuable when they interact and engage. The committed followers are gold. They are going to be your key customer-followers, and they are influencers. If you want to do something nice for some of your customers, the ones that are your influencers and brand ambassadors are the ones to start with, because you will get the most back from them.

But how do you know which followers are customer-followers? In Part Two, we'll look at a few tools to help you with finding out.

4.3 IDENTIFYING NEEDS, TASTES, AND "LIKES"

In order to attract the browsers, maintain customers, and entice your followers, you need to address their particular needs, tastes, and likes. This means you first have to find out what their needs, tastes, and likes are.

A *need* is linked to a particular problem to be solved or concern to be addressed. It is a pain point, which you can hopefully remove for your target audience. In order to showcase properly what you've got, you will need to pitch your content and represent your product or service so that

Shared Value

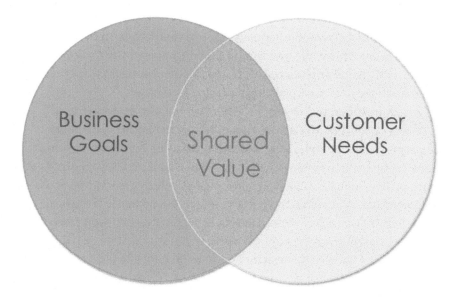

people can easily see how it addresses their needs or concerns. In most cases, it makes sense to make this as obvious as possible, so that the relevance of your product or service gets noticed and you can move directly from being viewed to being patronized. Ask yourself then: What particular problem does my enterprise solve? What concern does it address for my audience? Make sure your social media content reflects this. If your business goals and your customer needs are aligned, you have created shared value, because both business and customer needs are being met. Find this sweet spot, and you will most easily convert browsers into customers and customers into influencers.

Strive to find the shared value between your business and your customers' needs.

As in every other aspect of marketing in the two-way-conversation social media universe, identifying needs and concerns is not a one-way or top-down activity. It is conversational and interrelational. Don't assume that you know in advance exactly what need or concern your product or service addresses. You need to go online and see how (if at all) people are talking about you; see how they are representing themselves using what you offer; it may not fit in with your own initial understanding. You can also find out to what extent people may be complaining about what you do or unfavorably comparing it to a competitor. In each case, and as a general principle, you should take the opportunity to directly engage with actual or potential users and ask them outright what need or concern they use your product or service to address.

Tastes are different from needs. Whereas a need arises from a lack, problem, or concern, like an itch that needs scratching, a taste is more about preference or style. Two people may have similar needs—say they need to buy a stereo system for their car—but may have two very different taste-profiles: one likes classical music, one likes heavy metal. You probably won't sell a car stereo to a guy who likes classical music if you have a video clip of a bunch of metal heads banging their heads to loud heavy metal music while driving around in a car.

A *"like"* is a peculiarly social media phenomenon; like the status of being a *follower*, it encompasses a hybrid of lukewarm half-interest with seriously wanting to know everything as it happens. By and large, the "like" is a Facebook phenomenon. When people on Facebook like your page, their engagements with your page can be shared with their friends, and may even prompt their friends to like your page too, and so on with the friends of their friends and *their* friends too. The potential for exponential exposure is of the essence of the Facebook "like."

You need to do something to make liking your page worthwhile. Incentivize your likes, so that people will keep engaging with your page, and their activity will be publicized to their friends. Contests, questions, or a chance to participate in a big company decision may help keep people engaged. Keep the page updated, advertise sales and/or discounts, and offer exclusive content. Share funny cat videos with them, and educate them about your offers and partner offers. By providing value and reasons for people to actually *like* your company when they "like" your company page, you will motivate people to move from being luke-warm lazy browser-type followers to being full-blown fan followers and recurrent customers.

You need actively to court likes, just like you would court a potential mate. Remind people to like you on your website (you can even make a direct link) on the signature file of any emails you send, and on any other promotional material you put out into the world—but most of all give them a reason to like you and return to your content often.

4.4 TARGETING DEMOGRAPHICS

In the first section of this chapter, we mentioned a whole nest of questions to pose about your audience so you could fine-tune your content and specifically direct your interactions to particular kinds of people. For example, we mentioned: What are their concerns and values? What values do they share with you or your business? What benefits are they looking for? What do they like? Who are their friends? Where do they live (in the city, suburbs, or countryside)? What is their age, income, gender, ethnicity, relationship status, and sexual orientation? Are they politically conservative or liberal? Do they have a lot of siblings? What are their dietary preferences, hobbies, and passions?

One subset of such considerations is traditionally more of a focal point than others, and that is the subset of characteristics grouped under the label demographics. Demographics is the study of quantifiable large-scale groupings in a population. Especially relevant to social media marketing, the root word is *demos*, which means "people" in ancient Greek. Roughly speaking, targeting demographics is an important way to make sure that you make your product or service dependably appealing to large swaths of the population who tend to behave in quantitatively predictable ways.

If you have ever been interviewed on the phone by a public opinion researcher, you know from the questions they ask you that the main demographic categories are age, gender, race, ethnicity, income, home ownership status, disability, and employment status. In your social media marketing, such broad distinctions are helpful to keep in mind when you craft your content and image. Just like you probably wouldn't try to sell engagement rings to married men, you probably won't be enticing an unemployed single mother of three who can't afford to buy a house with any content that tries to attract people into buying accessories for an off-road dirt bike. On the other hand, the risk of demographics is the pitfall of stereotyping; in this day and age, even if you target demographic is a 20-something woman, if she lives in a progressive big city like San Francisco, Chicago, or New York City, you might actually end up alienating her by relying on traditionally "girly" content (e.g., pink colors, kitty cats, and dinnerware you can use to serve your husband when he gets home).

It's important to understand that while social media purports to be all about community and consumer empowerment, its very success as a new communication medium piqued the interest of marketers and businesses like you and me. We are eager to target customers where they are, whether it be when they are watching a big event like the Super Bowl on television, or just connecting with friends on Facebook. For social channels to continue to offer their services to their users, they must remain profitable. Therefore, the bigger social channels offer advertising to businesses in order to continue growing their own businesses. I bring this up here, because one glance at all the various demographic and interest-targeting options on Facebook may give you a new perspective on just how much data mining is occurring, and, more importantly, how valuable demographic and interest targeting is.

For example, in the figure below you will see that on Facebook we can advertise by city (within 10, 25 or 50 miles radius), state, country, language, age range, gender, as well as by specific interests and behaviors. The option to target so specifically affords increased ability to actually reach your intended customer instead of just someone with a similar demographic profile. We will delve deeper into this in Part Two.

Opposite is a screenshot of Facebook's advertising platform for promoting page likes. Notice the Audience Definition meter in the top right corner and all of the various options. Notice that without any targeting (i.e., just "United States"), we have a potential reach of 180,000,000 people. If we change the targeting to just San Francisco, we would reach 2,200,000. Then, refine to people ages 25–45, and the number goes down to 1,200,000. Next, just to women, and the number becomes 560,000. What if we just want to reach employees at Google? There are 2,400 of them. And what if we just want all women, ages 25–45, in San Francisco, who are interested in meditation (not just Google employees)? The number goes up to 28,000. With Facebook's targeting you can be very specific about which audience you reach with ads.

The Facebook Advertising Setup Dashboard. *Source:* www.facebook.com[14]

4.5 DEVELOPING TARGET-SPECIFIC CONTENT

Imagine you have a new love interest. What do you do to make them smile? First, you find out what things they like, what they find funny or interesting, the kind of flowers they like or perhaps their favorite food or chocolate. If you know these things it is much easier to win that smile and start building your relationship. The same applies in social media. You have to know your audience so well that you know how to make them smile, laugh, cry, and applaud you.

Remember, you want your social media audience to regard your online persona as someone they trust, want to engage with, and want to hang out with. So you need to make sure you present your persona as sharing common interests with your potential and existing customers. In this regard, taste is particularly important in the social media universe. Beyond the usual things like taste in music and movies, you can consider food (if you are selling a grill in a town like Berkeley, for example, where there are a lot of vegetarians, show pictures of grilling vegetables, not grilling carcasses), color schemes, and the like. The precise range of relevant matters of taste will depend on exactly what your product or service is. In general, a question of taste may determine whether or not a potential customer or follower becomes a customer or a repeat customer (i.e., a customer-follower). The product might do exactly what they want it to do, but if it doesn't come in the right shade of turquoise, then some people just might not be interested.

The first step in developing target-specific content is to understand what you are offering and how it fulfills the needs of your potential customers. Unfortunately, just believing that we have the best product in the world is not enough. This is where an audit of your capabilities, values, and competition comes into play. You'll want to understand where you are in the marketplace, how many other companies are selling a similar product in your city, country, or the world that you will need to compete with. My colleague George Kao once said, "Remember there are no competitors, only teachers." Learn from your competitors. Study what is working for them and what they are struggling with. Figure out where their weaknesses are and see if you can be strong in those areas.

The second step in your quest to develop content that will be most appealing to your target is to build what I like to call a brand hero/ heroine. This is a fictitious person who embodies all the characteristics of a typical member of your target audience. This person loves your brand, will talk about your product positively online and offline and advocate for your brand without you even asking them to. You want to know everything about your brand hero/heroine. Think about them as you would of a potential life partner, because they are going to show you how to reach customers just like them, and they could be the difference between the long-term success or failure of your business. This person may be based off an existing customer who is already advocating for your brand, or you can develop a new brand hero/heroine. Give him or her a name so that you can talk about him or her in the first person. Describe all the attributes that make them your brand hero. These will range from general demographics such as age, gender, and geolocation to lifestyle characteristics, attitude, character, and purchase habits.

For example, let's say we are a holistic medicine clinic wanting to recruit new patients. First, we want to define our brand hero/heroine. Let's say she is a 34-year-old highly active young professional living in San Francisco and working for Google. She is smart, interested in holistic health, and meditates daily. Common challenges she faces are stress and wanting to find a mate. She is constantly looking for healthy food choices and has an upbeat attitude, but is also concerned about the environment and poverty. She is a social drinker and likes rock climbing when she has time to get away. Her name is Jenna and she is very active on social media. Her favorite platforms are Google+, Facebook, and Twitter, and she has her own blog, where she writes about living in San Francisco and healthy choices. That's a lot we know about Jenna. Do you think we will be able to develop content specifically for her? So do I.

The Super Bowl 2015 Esurance commercial provides a good analogy of how silly it is to lump people into general demographic categories (watch http://bit.ly/sortaMom). Know your audience, and tailor content to them as specifically as possible.

Sorta Your Mom

Esurance ☑

▶ Subscribe   4,654

1,297,048

Sorta Your Mom Esurance ad for Super Bowl 2015. *Source:* www.youtube.com[15]

4.6 THINK AND ACT LIKE YOUR CUSTOMER

Now it's time to think and act like your customer. This follows from our first axiom of the laws of the social media universe: It is a two-way conversation, with many-to-many interactions. For this reason, you need to appear to your customer as someone like them, and you need to engage them on their level, not from above. One easy way to do this is to practice engaging in what sociologists call "perspective taking," or what ordinary people call "putting yourself in somebody else's shoes." Take a moment to put yourself in the position of your target audience and your actual customers. How would you want to be treated and addressed in your social media interactions? You will recognize this as a version of the golden rule: "Do unto others as you would have others do unto you." This is more important than ever in the social media universe.

If your audience, customers, and buyers don't feel like you are treating them with respect, they can very easily make a big deal out it: They can post negative comments about you on Yelp, they can create an angry video and post it on YouTube where it might be seen thousands or millions of times, and they can endlessly troll your Facebook page or Comments section on your blog. It's easier to focus on winning customers if you're not trying to clean up your reputation. Therefore, practice putting yourself in the perspective of your customer and guiding your own actions so as to satisfy and engage them. If you succeed at treating them well, like they are treated by their friends and family, you can reap the benefits of customer loyalty: Think about positive comments on your pages, positive Yelp reviews, happy customer videos on YouTube, and so on.

Thinking and acting like your customer will make all of your interactions with them go more smoothly. If you perfect the skill of seeing yourself and your product or service from their perspective, your communications with them will flow more naturally and feel less scripted. You will know exactly what to say, rather than having to speak in banalities, clichés, and generalities. Your customers and buyers will notice, and this will motivate them to trust and respect you and keep coming back to you. The enthusiasm and trust you inspire in them will also become contagious. They will naturally express their affinity for your brand when talking about you to their friends and family, who will think, "Jeez, Jimmy really does like Company X, I should really check them out."

For example, my colleague Cariwyl Hebert recently told me that her sister-in-law, Cat, mentioned being excited to get home to Sacramento from a trip to San Francisco so that she could mop the floors. What? Yes, that was my thought exactly; however, Cariwyl proceeded to tell me that Cat had purchased a new kind of mop for hardwood floors that she just couldn't say enough good things about. At the time, I thought this a bit strange, but, soon after that conversation, I visited Cariwyl at her home and noticed that her floors were extremely shiny and clean. Not only that, but they were smooth and felt really good on the feet too. I asked her about her floors and she asked if had I noticed a difference. She told me she also had purchased the mop Cat had mentioned, and that it is amazing. That's the kind of conversation you want your brand heroine to have with you on social media. That's the kind of brand hero you want to connect with, understand, and provide interesting and engaging content for.

Since I didn't yet know the name of the mop, I Googled "hardwood floor mop" to see what would come up, but couldn't exactly pinpoint which one it might be from the results I got. There is no shortage of options. So what's my next course of action? I texted Cariwyl and she responded with "It's a Bissel Power Fresh. Will send a photo. It's great!"

People are much more likely to trust recommendations they get from their friends than advertising from a big brand. Especially in social media, you want your content to get into the mindset of your customer as a friend. The more you can treat your customer just as you would treat a friend, the more likely they will be to return the favor and share your offers with their friends. Of course, this is never going to work if you have a bad product, but if your product is good and you put yourself in your customer's shoes, addressing their needs and putting them first, you are poised to do well in the social media universe.

When I talk about developing a social media plan in my classes I always ask my students the following question: "What are relationships made of?" They usually come up with several good answers, like trust, companionship, respect, and even lust. The answer I want them to give, though, is love. Relationships are made of love, and in social media the word "LOVE" spells out a plan for you. That is:

Listen
Offer
Visit
Engage

You can't have a conversation without listening, so make listening your first priority. If you love someone, you also want to offer them something. Think about Valentine's Day when you give someone flowers or chocolates. Even just making a good referral to a friend is offering them something of value. You also can't have a relationship without visiting another person is some way. You need to visit them in order to get to know them and form a bond. And, finally, once you have reached the point that you are bonded, you want to keep them engaged by continuing to provide value to the relationship and build trust and respect.

Your Social Media Plan

LOVE

L - Listen
O - Offer
V - Visit
E - Engage

Your Social Media Plan is LOVE. Listen—Offer—Visit—Engage. *Photo Credit:* Christina Ditzel

4.7 CREATING FANDOM

We distinguished between browsers, customers, and followers, and saw how the most coveted goal is a repeat and loyal customer who is also a follower. But from there we can actually go up another notch; we don't want to produce mere loyalty. We want to produce fanaticism in our customers. We want them to love our brands like Lady Gaga's fans love her (and like Britney Spears and Madonna's fans loved them in their time). We want them to wear shirts and hats with our logo on them. We want them to be so enthused that they talk about us without our having to prompt them; that they come to our defense whenever we are attacked by trolls.

How do we create these kinds of fans? The answer is simple: Act like Lady Gaga, and be awesome. Be adventurous and, every now and then, be a little outrageous (in a demographically appropriate manner, of course). Stand out. Reach out to your individual customers. Make them feel special. Show them how much you love creating your product for or delivering your service to them. Create contests for them and give stuff (free downloads, special editions of your product, etc.) to them as prizes. Give stuff to them for nothing and out of nowhere sometimes too. Incorporate their input into what you do. Create a Twitter hashtag and get your fans to use it and spread it around. All of these things and more will help cement you as a rock star of the social media universe, one able to create devoted fans out of recurrent customers and irregular buyers.

Remember the hardwood floor mop I mentioned in the previous section? Well, it just so happens that Bissel has been using several of these tactics on Facebook. Their engagement level is waning, though. How do we know? Take a look at their LikeAlyzer score and recommendations and you'll see. Yes, you *should* try this at home. Go to www.likealyzer.com for tips on how to improve your Facebook page. You might also want to enter your competitors' Facebook pages into the LikeAlyzer tool in order to better understand how they are doing. Enjoy!

One of Bissell's best-performing posts on Facebook is a contest. Notice the #PetHappens hashtag they created for it. A sample report from http://keyhole.co for just the week of 2/07/2015 through 2/15/2015 shows they received 209 posts by 153 people, for a total reach of 1,904,088 and 1,932,388 impressions.

BISSELL
January 2 ·

Pets are notorious mess makers, and we want to hear your stories! Share your best pet story on Twitter or Instagram using #PetHappens from now until February 15 and we'll donate $1 to BISSELL Pet Foundation, up to $50,000!

PUTTING THE WORST OF
PET MESSES
TO THE BEST OF USE.

#PetHappens

Share your pet story on Twitter or Instagram using #PetHappens to trigger a $1 donation to the BISSELL Pet Foundation® (up to $50,000).

Pet Happens

Now through February 15, 2015 share your messiest pet story on Twitter or Instagram using #PetHappens to trigger a $1 donation (up to $50,000) to BISSELL Pet Foundation—an organization dedicated to helping pets find forever homes.

BISSELL.COM

Like · Comment · Share · 👍 3,555 💬 55 ➦ 93

Bissell had success with it's #PetHappens campaign. *Source:* www.facebook.com[16]

The Facebook page itself may have a few issues, one of which may include the need for a community manager who is more responsive to the fans and people posting, especially on the weekend. For example, there are no responses from the company about complaints placed this weekend. It may well happen that they respond by Monday, but for any potential customers looking at their page over the weekend, this lack of responsiveness does not convey a good message.

Grace Dressler ▶ BISSELL

February 14 · 🌐

I bought a new Bissell vacuum several months ago at Walmart. It is the WORST vacuum I have ever owned. Dust and dirt shoots out of the bottom of the vacuum and now it has very little suction. I searched online and found that many others have had the same problems YET you continue to sell the vacuum knowing that it is defective! I wanted to return it from the start BUT you only allow customers to return it directly to you, as opposed to returning it to Walmart which is much easier. Its unacceptable that I should have to ship such a large item,, wait for repair, refund etc- I should be able to simply return it to Walmart. Perhaps you purposely make it difficult so customers don't return it?

Ruth O'Steen Lineberger ▶ BISSELL

February 14 · Tampa, FL · 🌐

Been trying to talk to someone via your customer service 800-237-7691 number, HOWEVER it just circles and circles me with an automated voice giving me unrelated options to choose from. VERY frustrated and disappointed. Bad job 😞

Like · Comment · Share · 💬 1

An example of a complaint posted on the weekend. The company is not responding on the weekend.
Source: www.facebook.com[17]

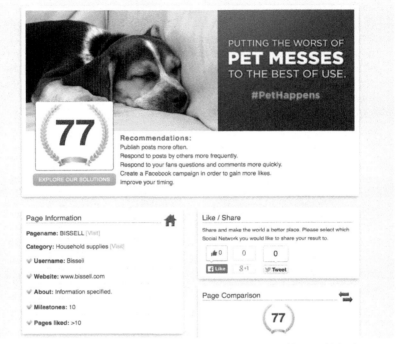

Review of BISSELL

PUTTING THE WORST OF
PET MESSES
TO THE BEST OF USE.

#PetHappens

77

Recommendations:
Publish posts more often.
Respond to posts by others more frequently.
Respond to your fans questions and comments more quickly.
Create a Facebook campaign in order to gain more likes.
Improve your timing.

EXPLORE OUR SOLUTIONS

Page Information

Pagename: BISSELL [Visit]

Category: Household supplies [Visit]

Username: Bissell

Website: www.bissell.com

About: Information specified.

Milestones: 10

Pages liked: >10

Like / Share

Share and make the world a better place. Please select which Social Network you would like to share your result to.

👍 0   0   0

Like   8+1   Tweet

Page Comparison

77

LikeAlyzer by Meltwater will provide you with a score for your Facebook page. Use this as a guideline from which to make changes. *Source:* www.likealyzer.com[18]

CHAPTER 5

WORD OF MOUTH

5.1 WORD OF MOUTH: WHAT IS IT?

Word of mouth, like the word on the street, is an old-fashioned way of spreading information and evaluations. People are by nature communicative beings; we can't help talking to each other about the things that please us as well as the things that bother us. We are also by nature cooperative beings; no one individual knows everything there is to know about everything in the world, so we just have to rely on others for learning things. We have to trust the value judgments of others (especially experts or other people we are predisposed to trust), since there is not enough time in our individual lives to arrive on our own at well-founded judgments about everything relevant to us. Additionally, we now live in the era of information overload, which requires a lot of filtering. Some of this filtering happens through our choices of friends and the media we consume.

Our communicative nature doesn't just enable us to describe the world to each other; it enables and inclines us to recommend things to each other, and it feeds our natural tendencies to imitate each other and to rely on the advice and examples of one another. These are the roots of the power of word of mouth. We tend to listen to the music being listened to by the people around us and those whose opinion we trust; we tend to buy the bottle of wine we overhear other people enthusiastically praising; we develop mistrust for the administrators being spoken negatively about by other people we know.

In face-to-face interactions, we also use facial expressions, tone of voice, and other accoutrements of in-person communication to help us convey emphasis, mood, and evaluation. People have always been gossip mongers, a tendency greatly amplified by the emergence of widely distributed newspapers in the 19th century, then again with cable television in the 1980s and 1990s. And since the core of gossip is sharing, the tendency toward gossip and sharing stories through word of mouth was elevated to new and unforeseen heights by the spread of social media. Stories and words from numerous mouths can now circulate virtually and instantly all around the world. This has radically changed the extent of the influence of word of mouth on the success and failure of brands, products, and services.

Traditional marketing strategies, the ones in place prior to the social media revolution, relied mostly on straightforward, one-way advertising (billboards, magazine and newspaper ads, commercials on TV). Even though they hoped that these avenues would also open up word-of-mouth effects, it wasn't obvious to them how to systematically create influence and spread word of mouth. Social media provides the path, a direct avenue for you to reach your customers with your words, and for customers to spread the message about your product among their friends and followers.

One of my alma mater Oberlin College's key marketing slogan used to be: "All roads lead to Oberlin." This meant that, no matter where you came from before attending college there, your life's journey had brought you there as a prospective student for a reason. This is also the case for word of mouth: There are several different roads that word of mouth travels upon. First of all there is the road that leads from you to the public. Then there is the road among the public that goes between different audiences or customers and potential customers. To understand which roads your fans are on, you need to find out who is already sharing the content you produce, and be sure you can keep making it easily available to them. Remember "fish where the fish are"? But how do you find out? Take a look at www.socialmention.com and type in your brand name (you may need to do this in quotes to refine or specify your search). SocialMention.com will tell you how many mentions have been made about your brand recently, and also where most people are talking about

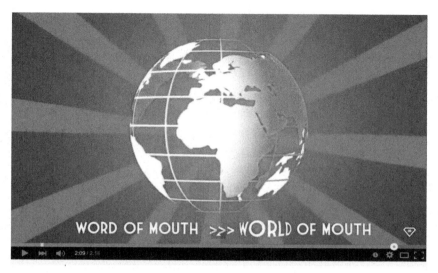

Social Media Revolution 2015 #Socialnomics

equalman

▶ Subscribe 466

106,919

"Word of mouth has become World of mouth." —Erik Qualman. *Source:* www.youtube.com[19]

you. This helps you find out what particular format of content is being shared most widely, so you can focus on producing that: is it audio (like podcasts), written texts (like blog posts or quizzes), or visual content (either still pictures, memes, or short videos)? The fact that you can also make content that is sharable across multiple platforms, thereby reaching more people and putting more words in more mouths and on the street more efficiently, is what Erik Qualmann refers to as "World of Mouth." See @Equalman's most recent Youtube overview of the state of Social Media at http://bit.ly/equalw0m.

For example, a video uploaded to YouTube can be shared in a tweet, and a screen capture or brief clip from it can be shared on Instagram and Vine.

Another key issue is identifying the people out there on social media who are influential in a given domain (e.g., resort hotels) who you want to appeal to, or who just have a lot of friends and connections. You want to get your content into the hands of the influencers, because if someone with 10,000 or a million followers shares something, that is way more effective for you than if 20 people with 150 friends each share your content. It is not just the people with the most followers whose mouths you want to get your words into, but also people who are the most passionate and the most intrinsically motivated to go out there and share and talk about your stuff. And sometimes these people will have fewer followers than the top industry influencers, but their cult passion can be just as effective or even more so. These are your super fans.

How do you find influencers and super fans? You can research your competitors to see who their influencers and top fans are; you can do blog searches, search hashtags, search YouTube, and look at a tool like www.SocialMention.com again to understand what people are saying about you, your competitor, your industry, and/or your product. You can also hire other companies to locate the influencers and the passionate sharers for you. These word-of-mouth generators are your brand ambassadors. They become truly taken by what you do, and may even start their own community centered around your product or service, like the Coke Facebook page from 2009, which had the second highest number of fans (after Barack Obama) and wasn't started by anyone employed by the Coca-Cola company (see http://adage.com/article/digital/coke-fans-brought-brand-facebook-fame/135238/).

The foundation of inciting word-of-mouth buzz about you is, of course, having an excellent product or service that people can genuinely and wholeheartedly share with and recommend to their friends, followers, and family. You also obviously need to treat your customers well, make them feel valued and heard (and not taken for granted), and you should reward return customers' and repeat customers' loyalty. If you have to give stuff away or do something else to motivate influencers and other people to open the word-of-mouth channels about your enterprise, go for it—just make sure you have researched what each person is willing to accept. For example, Sue Ann Gleason of Chocolate for Breakfast states: "My chocolate palate is pretty sophisticated so please don't send me cheap chocolate. I won't sample it. And please don't tell me about its oxygen radical absorption capacity. That is NOT how I choose my chocolates." (See www.chocolateforbreakfast.com/about/.)

If you do give stuff away to people in order to help motivate them to write about you in their blog, talk about you in their podcast, or feature you in one of their funny YouTube videos, it is absolutely crucial that you require them to disclose the fact that they have received things from you. Word of mouth can go from positive to negative really fast, and anything that reeks of manipulation or subterfuge can be discovered way more easily than you might think, and it can easily ruin your reputation. Stick to the rule of honesty and transparency about what you give away and to whom. Signaling this will not at all invalidate the endorsements or recommendations you receive, if those in turn are heartfelt and real; on the contrary, it will help cement the sense that your product is "the real deal." The most important thing in word of mouth is to provide the best service that you possibly can and to come across as real. If you do this, people will feel comfortable and ready to share what you've done. Your goal here is to inspire conversations and to set the context so they can spread and recur.

Also, if you learn of someone who is talking about you in a positive light, be polite and thank them. Not only will you get another mention in the social media universe, but you will also generate a good feeling from the original influencer, and they will be much more likely to say good things about you again.

5.2 WORD OF MOUTH: WHY IS IT MORE EFFECTIVE?

It is easy to see why word of mouth is more effective than traditional marketing in the context of the social media universe. Social media is social and word of mouth is social too. This is just to say that people trust recommendations that come from their friends and family (or other people they defer to or rely on or antecedently trust) way more than they trust some ad created by an advertising agency, which we all know is just trying to get your attention and entice you in ways you can't fully trust.

Moreover, we trust other consumers to be honest about the companies and services they use more than we trust the people who provide the service. Look at the enormous popularity of the reviews section on

Amazon or Yelp as exhibit A for this claim. Even though Yelp's program of pulling out negative reviews for a fee, or their reported suppressing of positive reviews for companies who don't pay, somewhat undermines the credibility of its service, this does not take away from the fact that we want to know what other users and customers have to say about their experience with a certain brand, store, product, or service. One of my clients recently quoted someone as saying "You live and die by the sword of Yelp," and unfortunately this can often be true.

Of course, the improved efficacy of word-of-mouth marketing does not happen automatically. You need to help enable it by paying attention to the things mentioned above (like finding and motivating the influencers, providing an awesome product or service, being grateful to your fans, etc.). But there is also the issue of timing. Because of the temporal immediacy of social media, good timing is essential. The pace of events is vastly accelerated in the social media universe. Everything there happens so fast and people respond instantaneously, so content can grow stale or become inappropriate very quickly. You need to make the instantaneous nature of social media interactions work to your advantage. We will discuss this issue further in the next chapter.

For now, we can at first recommend that you publish your content at a time when most of your target audience is online. There are many tools which make it easy for you to find out when that is. The timing consideration is becoming looser now that smart phones have become ubiquitous and people check their social media accounts several times an hour, but we can still confidently assert that publishing content in the middle of the night is probably not the best strategy (unless, for example, you are trying to reach a European audience and you happen to be in the United States, or you want to grow your Twitter followers globally, and thus the best way is to post often throughout the day). Dan Zarrella, in his 2013 book *The Science of Marketing: When to Tweet, What to Post, How to Blog, and Other Proven Strategies,* found that "followers peaked with accounts that tweeted around 22 times per day and there was no steep drop off after that." Publish your content in the morning, loading the good stuff for early in the week (and test to see whether or not publishing important missives on Sundays will be beneficial), so that the content has the whole week ahead of it to spread down the word-of-mouth avenues.

Another thing you can do is to take advantage of holidays or current events to publish relevant content, perhaps even taking care to find obscure or entertaining marginal holidays or remembrances to give your content an edge. Everyone is going to publish something special on Christmas and New Year's. Maybe you should publish some specially tailored content on National Avocado Appreciation Day?

CHAPTER 6

INTRO TO SOCIAL MEDIA

6.1 ONE-TO-ONE VS. MANY-TO-MANY COMMUNICATION: DIALOGUE WITH AND AMONG YOUR CUSTOMERS

What puts the social in "social media"? Dialogue and conversation, that's what. In the social media universe you cannot come off like you are on a monologue. Social media doesn't work as a broadcast platform. Your audience is wired in and they can and will respond directly to what you say. Therefore, you should always pitch your content as an opening move in a dialogue, and be ready to listen well and respond respectfully. You will need to have an empathetic connection with your audience, and you need to understand them; it is not enough to describe and pitch your products and services to them, you need to see and respond to their needs and interests, and show them in an interactive way how your offer can help them. Your aim is to talk *with* them, not to them and not at them. This is harder than it sounds. In traditional marketing, as exemplified by billboards, magazine ads, or television commercials, companies engage in one-way communication: talking to or at their potential customers. In such cases, the customers are direct objects, rather than being subjects and co-creators of the communication process. Conversely, in social media marketing, the communication is multidirectional, not one way.

With reference to database relational programming, I like to call this many-to-many versus one-to-many marketing, as many-to-many and one-to-many aptly refer to the different numbers of parties involved in the communication transaction. To call it many-to-many communication is to point out that you are always on the hook for being receptive and responsive to your audience; you want to provide them with content that will inspire them to say something back to you by leaving comments, sharing your content, or starting up a conversation with their own friends and social network about what you are doing. You want to listen to their needs and respond appropriately. This two-way dialogue is known as engagement.

If you don't respond to your audience, they will be talking among themselves anyway, and they will probably talk about how lame you are for not engaging in the conversation with them! Your task is to be responsibly responsive to them and thereby also to motivate them to engage in conversations among themselves too. It is not only a conversation between you and selected customers that you want your content to incite, it is a conversation that happens between you and your customers who are also conversing among themselves, thereby generating new interest and new engagements with you in turn. If you play this just right, you can generate a recurring "virtuous cycle" in which the online dialogue takes on a life of its own and pulls you along with it, without you actually having to be the leader and organizer or focal point of the conversation. This is what we mean by a "many-to-many" conversation.

Traditional advertising and marketing is about screaming for attention, not about engaging in conversations. Traditional advertising is about changing perceptions and is interruptive. Ads on the TV interrupt the show you are enjoying, the print ads break up the text in a newspaper or magazine, billboards are designed to catch your attention while you are supposed to be focused on driving, and junk mail never feels welcome when you open your mailbox. Most of the time such attempts to hook your attention are flashy and often obnoxious. These interruptions are seldom oriented toward starting a conversation, but rather intended to make an impression on the consumer that hopefully will be imprinted in their memory or subconscious mind. That's why with traditional marketing we often refer to top-of-mind awareness. That's why the candy bars are close to the checkout stand at the grocery store, because what you have seen most recently is more likely to be something you will consider purchasing next. Many-to-many communications, on the other hand, don't rely on imprints or impressions, because by inciting an ongoing conversation, your product or service will remain organically in your audience's field of attention and awareness for a prolonged period of time.

Super Bowl 2015 was a few weeks ago. Advertisers pay millions of dollars for a spot during the Super Bowl because of the sheer number of people who will watch it. Mostly, these people (unless they are marketers or advertising professionals) are watching for the game of football. The ads are often thought of as the biggest ads of the year for each advertiser, yet the unfortunate truth is that many of the ads don't live on in the minds of the huge audience watching, because many viewers are distracted by lots of other input, such as food, drinks, football fandom, and friends.

For the amount of money it takes to air a single ad on the Super Bowl, your company could hire a whole team of social media managers to work on building content and engaging with your customers and followers, and thus help spread the word about your company in a way that feels organic and not at all like broadcasting with a megaphone. Traditional marketing tends to want to knock the consumer over the head with the message, while social media invite the consumer to sit down and have a conversation instead. Which one do you prefer?

6.2 DEFINITION OF SOCIAL MEDIA

Backing up for a moment to focus on some basic definitions, "social media" is a label given to a style of web-based communication that invites and relies upon the interaction of its users. Social media is all about sharing and relationships of individuals and groups online. It is distinctively DIY or "do it yourself," because literally anyone with an Internet connection can participate in the activities of social media. The interactions can be carried out in words, images, audio, or video. It is important to point out that "social media" is not synonymous with "social networking." Social networking happens on sites such as Facebook, LinkedIn, and Twitter where people create a profile to represent themselves and to use as their "home base" for communications, and that is just one form that social media interactions take. Social media is a broader category including video-sharing sites like YouTube, Vine, and Vimeo; music-sharing sites and services like Bandcamp, Spotify, Pandora, and Rdio; blogs; wikis (with ongoing, user-generated content); photo-sharing sites and applications like Instagram, Pinterest, Flickr, and Photobucket; citizen journalism and news-sharing sites like Onpublico and Buzzfeed; dating sites like OkCupid, Match.com, HER, Grindr, and Tinder; and messaging services like Snapchat and WhatsApp.

As mentioned in the introduction, there are two primary features of social media, which we dubbed the laws of the social media universe. These are *interactivity* and *immediacy*.

Interactivity means that people use social media for connecting with others, sharing stories and gossip, having conversations, exchanging information, and so on. Marketing on social media needs to be dialed in to their interactivity.

The immediacy of social media has to do with the instantaneous timing of events. When something happens in the world, it is being immediately tweeted about, blogged about, posted about in a status update, and so on.

To illustrate this, remember when Captain C. B. "Sully" Sullenberger landed a plane on the Hudson River in January 2009? The first news of this event was via Twitter by an ordinary citizen who posted a photo he took on his way to the rescue. That photo was then spread around the world by the media.

Just as digital photography has made everyone a photographer, social media has made everyone a journalist. The fact that social media facilitates citizen journalism and super-fast mass distribution is true not only for the most trivial events (witness the people who cannot eat any food without posting a picture of it on Instagram), but for more significant and momentous events as well, such as the anti-government protests in Egypt that ultimately brought down the Mubarak regime. These events were largely mobilized by sharing information on Twitter and Facebook. One of Erik Qualman's Social Media Revolution videos even quips that babies are being named Twitter and Facebook due to these platforms' role in the regime change. Because of social media's immediacy, you

 **Jānis Krūms**
@jkrums

http://twitpic.com/135xa - There's a plane in the Hudson. I'm on the ferry going to pick up the people. Crazy.

↩ 🔁 ⭐ •••

RETWEETS
204

FAVORITES
824

12:36 PM - 15 Jan 2009

Jānis Krūms's tweet about his photo of plane that landed in the Hudson River. *Source:* www.twitter.com[20]

Jānis Krūms's photo of the plane that landed in the Hudson River. *Source:* www.twitpic.com[21]

should always be on the lookout for how current events might make your product or service needed or relevant to your customers or potential customers. Social media gives you the ability to target your customers' needs and desires directly and exactly at the right time.

In short, social media sites are gathering places. People gather together to share things, learn, and engage in conversations regarding things that are important to them. Of course, any user of social media also knows that there is a lot of triviality and trolling that goes on too; people of older generations (usually age 40 and above) have a hard time seeing past all of the noise and BS that tends to go on in the social media universe. This is indeed one of the main challenges for the future of social media: How to control, sort through, and contain all the triviality, nonsense, and senseless bickering that it undeniably invites. This is where filtering is necessary and how the four C's of social media marketing (creating, curating, connecting, and culture) are replacing traditional marketing's four P's (product, place, price, promotion) (see bit.ly/equalw0m).

Those companies that are most successful at social media are the ones that understand their audience, love the medium, and have a unique personality with a strong dose of passion. As Brian Solis stated in "Participation Is Marketing," you cannot expect to have success with social media unless you are indeed participating on the social networks, engaging in conversations, sharing content, building your followers and fans, and being an active participant on all the channels where your audience is congregating.

Social media is indeed social sharing of consumer-generated content both with the media and by the new media, that is to say by us, you and me, regular everyday people. As Dan Gillmor aptly forecast in his 2006 book *We the Media: Grassroots Journalism, By the People, For the People*, "Success on Facebook happens, all of the time. But like with any successful relationship you need to put the time and effort into it to make it work. People, technology, and the world are constantly changing around us. Facebook needs to keep up by constantly changing, and that means as a business you have to as well."

6.3 CATEGORIES OF SOCIAL MEDIA

As mentioned in the introduction of the book, as illustrated by The Conversation Prism (www.conversationprism.com) there are many more social media sites than the big six that most people think of when they hear the term "social media" today, i.e. Facebook, Twitter, LinkedIn, Google+, Instagram, Pinterest, and YouTube.

The main categories of social media are: social networking sites, blogs, image-sharing sites, video-sharing sites, music-sharing sites, dating sites, social bookmarking sites, wikis, question/answer sites, message boards, listservs, and location-specific mobile applications. There are also several tools for listening and monitoring conversations that are particularly useful for understanding what people are saying about you. We'll discuss these in a later chapter.

Now we will briefly characterize each category of social media.

Social Networking sites are sites where users make a profile (with a greater or lesser degree of personalization) in order to share links, photos, messages, and generally to stay in touch with each other. Examples are Facebook, Twitter, LinkedIn, and Google+.

Blogs are personal webpages or sites authored by subject matter experts, normally with some very simple visual themes, whose point is to directly share personal content or expert reflections. A few well-known services, such as Blogspot, Blogger, and Wordpress, provide a ready-to-use template in which users can fill in their content. Livejournal is another option, and Tumblr is a burgeoning alternative to full-blown blogging, which serves as more of a mash-up between a microblogging tool like Twitter and an image-sharing platform like Instagram, along with the ability to write more text as you would in a blog.

Image-Sharing sites are exactly what they sound like: places where users post images for others to see. The dominant forces in image-sharing are Instagram (which was recently reported to have more active users than Twitter—Instagram with 300,000 and Twitter with 288,000 at the time of this writing) and Pinterest, but some others include Flickr, Photobucket, Snapchat, and Tumblr.

Video-Sharing sites are where you can find videos, YouTube being the dominating presence in this category, with Vimeo also being relevant.

Vine is a video-sharing service that focuses on short clips or loops, and Instagram offers 15-second video clips as well.

Music-Sharing sites are becoming something of a phenomenon too, now that the streaming of music is slowly overtaking the purchasing of music. Spotify makes it easy for people to be "friends" and to share playlists, etc. Other music-sharing sites of note are Pandora and Rdio.

Dating sites such as OkCupid and Match.com are becoming more and more popular every year. On these sites, users create a profile, upload images, and compose texts, and they also answer questions and quizzes to gauge their compatibility with other users. Tinder is fast becoming the matching site du jour. Grindr is specifically for gay men, and HER is a new dating app for lesbians.

Social Bookmarking sites such as Reddit, StumbleUpon, and Digg are places where users share, organize, and rank links to various pages and online content. Delicious is still being used, and Buzzfeed is big among millennials.

Wikis are sites that encourage and allow for user-generated and edited content. In principle, anyone is allowed to contribute to a wiki (though, of course, in some cases, restrictions exist).

Question/Answer sites like Quora, Blurtit, Romio, and Jelly offer places for people to both ask and answer questions, which is sometimes better than the results you might get from a search engine, because the answers come from real human beings.

Message Boards and *Forums* are sites where like-minded people congregate to share ideas and discuss various topics. The discussions are organized into ongoing threads, which anyone can start and contribute to. These are particularly useful for learning and problem-solving, and are often frequented by programmers.

Listservs are basically email versions of chat rooms. Threads and discussions are transmitted and read through email.

Location-Specific Mobile Applications use the GPS systems that are now prevalent in smart phones to tag the location of users, adding another dimension of sharing and interactivity. Foursquare is an example of this; by tracking the location of its users it recommends particular shops, products, and services to them.

6.4 GOING VIRAL

"Going viral" is the phrase used to describe a situation in which some content spreads quickly and exponentially across the Internet by being shared by many people whose friends and connections in turn share it with their friends and connections, who in turn share it with their friends and connections, and so on and so forth, with all this happening rapidly in a short window of time. Going viral is the ultimate word-of-mouth buzz phenomenon, with all the spreading of the content happening organically (from user to user). It is difficult to know in advance what content you can provide that will trigger a viral contagion across the web. For this reason, it is important to try a few different kinds of content (videos, songs, memes, etc., that are funny, ironic, serious, and so on), and a few different seeding strategies: Get as many bloggers to notice, especially ones with a large readership; take to Twitter and try to get retweets from people who have lots of followers; and go into forums and chat rooms where people are discussing things and insert your content into their discussions.

Most importantly, you have to produce content that is worth sharing so that people will want to share it. Be provocative. Remember that sometimes things may go viral without your intending them to, and that there is a degree to which viral buzz is inherently out of your control once it gets going. It might be some content made by someone else and involving your product or service that ends up going viral, so it is important for you to monitor the web to see if you can find out a possible viral incident brewing. One thing you should do is create one or more Google Alerts for your company and for things relevant to your offer. Another option is Mention.com. Google Alerts and Mention.com send you an email when new relevant content pertaining to your search terms shows up on the web. If you detect a possible viral outbreak brewing, do what you can to promote it and make it more sharable and visible. Monitor the web for people who have a story about an experience with your company, and see if you can help get their content shared and spread around. There is nothing like a viral outbreak to generate recognition and new possibilities for your company.

It is also crucial to make your content easy to share on your blog and website. Include "share" buttons, so users can directly and immediately share the content without any hassle. Your webmaster or a developer can help you with this if you are unable to do it yourself. Another strategy is to monitor current events that might generate a viral response, and see if you can piggy-back your content on the gathering viral wave that may be spreading around with or without you. To see what's trending, look at www.popurls.com, or just review the trends area on Twitter. Be careful that you are not accused of hijacking the conversation with your interjection, though. It's better to be an active participant offering value in a viral event than someone who is obviously there just because there is a viral event happening.

6.5 WHY YOU WANT IT

Why should you start or continue using social media or invest more money, time, and effort into it?

A quick search on a tool like Google Alerts or SocialMention.com for your brand, product, your own name and/or the name of your CEO, or even just your industry, will provide instant guidance. There you will see how much you are being mentioned online, and what kinds of things people are saying and thinking about you and/or your company. If you see what you expect, you're in good shape. If you are surprised pleasantly by anything you find, you will also likely be able to make some quick decisions about which social networks are going to be best for you to participate in, because you'll understand where it is that most people are talking about your business in a positive light and how you may be able to jump into those conversations. If you see negative information being shared, you'll know that you need to do something to remedy those negative comments and posts. The best way to do that is to reach out to your network and ask them to share what they appreciate about you.

Say you're a restaurant owner with mostly great reviews and lots of repeat customers. One day someone posts a bad review on Yelp and then shares it on Facebook. The best thing you can do in this situation is reach out to your network with a request along the lines of "Thank you for your business and for frequenting our restaurant. We hope you are still enjoying our food. We sure do appreciate serving you. We have recently received a negative review which we don't believe is warranted, and it is causing a small amount of stress for our owners. If you have ever had a great experience with us and want to show your support, now is the time. Please share a review or post your thoughts on one of our social networks. We really appreciate your time and look forward to serving you again soon."

Of course you'll need to have already built your network and that would have taken you some time, but if you have done that and not asked for too much, you would likely get the support you needed and the small blip on your business résumé would be buried by positive comments.

Not only is social media good for having an army behind your cause, but it also helps your search engine rankings and provides more ways for your customers to connect with you. Do a search on Google for anything, and you'll find that the sites ranking the highest in the search results are those with the most significant social presence. That is because social media affords more links from high-authority sites such as Facebook, Twitter, and LinkedIn back to your site. High-authority inbound links to your site are extremely valuable from a search engine optimization standpoint, and if you're choosing to not be on social media, you will have seen a drop in your search engine–referred traffic to your website or blog over the past couple of years.

Also, consider where your audience spends most of their time online. Is it on your website, a search engine, or a social network? Since Facebook has more than a billion active users per month, chances are that most of your audience spends quite a bit of time on Facebook. Remember about fishing where the fish are? You want to be where your audience is, that's where the cocktail party is happening and where all your small connections and high-value conversations are started.

You shouldn't really be questioning why you want it, but, rather, where your audience is.

6.6 BEING OPEN 24/7

We've already mentioned the peculiar temporality of social media, that is, its immediacy. It is immediate because it is on all the time. Things are happening in social media whenever people are online talking about and sharing things, which is to say, constantly. This is both the danger and the opportunity, the blessing and the curse. It is dangerous because a story can get away from you quickly, without you having a chance to impact it, and because negative stories and content pertaining to your product or service can just as easily go viral as positive ones. But it is an opportunity for you at the same time: an opportunity for to you connect directly with your customers and potential customers, exactly when your offer is relevant to them.

Real-time marketing is becoming more and more prominent, with social media teams becoming more and more sophisticated at improvising and creating content on the fly. Jay Baer talks about how Real-Time Relevancy is key to your company's becoming a "Youtility" for your customers, because that is one of the ways to focus on help and not hype, (i.e., on adding value by being useful).

The Internet never closes or takes a break or goes to sleep. That means that you need always to be ready to engage with your audience and provide your service to them, and to connect with them when they want it or need it. Since negative reviews or news about you can also pop up at anytime, you always need to be on the lookout for those as well, and be ready to respond. People have become accustomed to the instantaneous nature of Internet communications, and this has caused a general erosion of patience. People hate waiting, now more than ever. Because they can always go on and look for something they want or need, you have to always be ready to provide it to them and to respond to their concerns, because if you don't, they may find what they are looking for in a timely manner from a competitor. Instantaneous responsiveness has become a norm of decency on today's social media universe. Your customers will be in turn providing you with constant feedback, which you can then act on, thus creating more satisfaction for them.

Of course, this doesn't mean that you have to be constantly on your social media sites, but you need to check them regularly, even at night and first thing in the morning. Being the first to respond to a major event in the world or even just in your business domain brings a huge advantage; people will associate you and your service with the events of the day. Social media responsiveness, then, is by its nature not very amenable to long-term rational planning. What it takes is a sense of adventure and spontaneity, both of which will be contagious and refreshing to your customers and audience. You might make more mistakes or missteps this way, but the good part is that you can correct them instantly too. Instantaneous responsiveness is, of course, not meant to replace longer-term planning based on research, but it is now an indispensible complement to more traditional strategies and planning. In short, have a plan and also be ready to improvise.

6.7 SOCIAL MEDIA INSTEAD OF A WEBSITE

The Internet has evolved in such a way that most people spend more time on social media sites than traditional websites. Websites are like the yellow pages of the Internet. Every now and then they are good to have around, but mostly we get by these days without having much to do with them at all. For this reason, it makes sense for you to focus your efforts on maintaining an active social media presence instead of a traditional website. This is not to say that you should give up on your website. You should have a place for people to land from a search or for more information after you have piqued their interest through your social media campaigns. However, a vibrant and engaging social media presence will be more of a hook for your future and present customers than a static, one-way traditional website. Your main website should always link back to your social media pages, and vice versa. Focus on providing high quality content and targeted information on the website. Make it a place your potential customers will want to spend some time at, make the information easily available and attractively displayed. Your website is a passive form of marketing; it's your storefront that is open 24/7; but you first have to get people to it before they can start learning more about you from there. Social media is how you get people to your website, and your website is where all of your evergreen content lives. Evergreen content is content which will be useful for a long period of time. Blogposts, infographics, and videos are good to embed on your website, because they provide additional reasons for search engines to rank your content highly when people are searching for topics that you have posted about. In search marketing, this kind of content is referred to as long-tail content, because it is available for indexing for a long time. Social posts, on the other hand, may be outdated very quickly, or may just not be indexable via a search engine because they are locked behind a privacy wall or login.

Websites are useful for posting special offers and breaking news. Give your customers a reason to bookmark your homepage because it offers interesting, entertaining, and/or valuable industry insights. Use your social media sites and posts to send them to your webpage, where you should make it as easy as possible for them to move through the sales cycle. The page should be kept simple, and the graphics should not be distracting. Make sure the site is mobile-friendly and fast-loading. Don't overwhelm your visitor with advertising. If a potential buyer has already landed on your site, help them complete their transaction with a strong call to action like "Buy" or "Book Now." The website should be designed for the buyer, with the buyer's perspective in mind; so remember, as we discussed earlier, to keep your target audience in mind, think of your brand hero/heroine and their particular demographics. That's who you're aiming to appeal to.

In sum, keep your website simple, a place where you can easily guide your customers through the completion of the buying cycle and give them any information they need, but focus more energy on social media on a day-to-day basis, because that is where you will be seen. Social media enables you to stay uppermost in the consciousness of your potential customer. And if you think of your customer as a friend and they feel the same way about you, your values will be aligned and you can be mutually beneficial to each other.

PART

2

CHAPTER 7

CHOOSING THE BEST SOCIAL MEDIA FOR YOUR PURPOSE

7.1 SHOULD YOU DROP OLD-STYLE MARKETING AND ONLY DO SOCIAL MEDIA?

Social media has already transformed the way people communicate. It is not going away, and we can only expect it to become ever more pervasive. Every person who is born into this world is now born into a digital world, a world in which social media is an integral part of everyday interactions. For these reasons, it may be tempting to predict that more people will be exposed to your company and brand if you focus on providing marketing through social media as opposed to traditional marketing tools such as billboards, commercials on TV and radio, magazine and newspaper advertisements, and so on. This is good thinking; however, it may not actually be wise unless you have a strong social media marketing strategy, a great team, and you can dedicate significant amounts of time and money to it.

If you're a small business, for example, you likely have a lot of responsibilities just running your business already. Do you have time to add another few hours a week to your existing role, or are you thinking, like many do, that you can just hire a student or an intern to do all the social media posting and community-building? If you are, please remember that interns still require lots of management and guidance, and there will need to be someone responsible for making sure the intern is acting, posting, and communicating just in the way you would hope to be doing with your customers.

If you have a large company and a substantial advertising budget, on the other hand, you can afford television commercials, billboards, and print advertising. These still get a lot of exposure, and can be targeted to your specific location. They still get reach: They appear in front of many people in your target audience. The real benefit of social media lies in its inherent nature of allowing you to be more personal and thus breed trust from your customers. Via social media, you can target much more specifically and grow your audience into loyalists. While people are becoming more and more resistant to traditional marketing media, their usage of and comfort with social media is steadily increasing. It's important to stay on top of this trend while also being realistic about it. If you can drop old-style marketing and focus on social media, then by all means do so, but make sure to keep your goals in mind, and start your social media marketing with the right attitude and planning behind it. If you are new to social media marketing and considering adding it to your promotional efforts, first answer the following questions for yourself and your business:

1. What is our story?
2. What is unique about our company that we can share in a positive, entertaining, or educational way on social media?
3. Who will be managing our social network accounts?
4. Do we have the resources to manage multiple social presences?
5. How much time (i.e. money) are we willing to spend on social media marketing?
6. Which social platforms are best for us?
7. Where does our audience hang out on in the social media universe?
8. Are we ready to generate lots of content?
9. What is it we are hoping to achieve?
10. Are we ready to be social?

To be effective in social media requires a lot of endurance, creativity, and time. All too often, people see other companies succeeding on social media and think that it must be free and easy. It is not free (unless you don't need to be paid for your time), and it requires constant planning, creating, monitoring, and nurturing. That's not to say it's not fun and fulfilling, but there is no easy fix or golden formulae to make you want to forget all about traditional media and focus only on social media.

Being present on social media is now as important as having a business card or a website, but it's just as important to understand where exactly you need to be most.

In this chapter we discuss the various major kinds of social media to help you determine which is the best one for you.

7.2 BLOGGING

The word "blog" comes from an abbreviation of the word "weblog," which was originally meant to be a log or journal of entries about one's life. Think of the *Diary of Anne Frank* in digital format, with her different entries appearing as different blog posts. Blogs have become an essential establishment in the social media universe. People trust blogs because they tend to feel more personal. Popular bloggers can have tremendous influence on public opinion. There is a blog for you on just about any topic of interest, since bloggers tend to be very focused around their particular niche.

Online audiences who may be skeptical of traditional advertising tend to view blogs as the authentic voice of a passionate individual or expert author, rather than a slick marketing ploy. A "hard sell" or something that reads as a press release can be a big turnoff for many potential customers, but a blog often represents a more personal voice or individual opinion, which readers can trust. A thoughtfully designed blog, with attention to overall style (think fonts, colors, and graphics, as well as content) has an independent rather than corporate feel. Readers often want to know about who the blogger is, so it may be a good idea to include some personal information about yourself (or whoever the author of the blog is), such as a photo, biography, or profile. While it's a great idea to personalize blogs, be sure to keep it ethical and accountable. That means being clear about who is actually doing the writing, disclosing your affiliations, giving credit where it is due, and considering privacy issues.

Audiences often find their way to blogs when they are searching for information or answers to specific questions. A well-written, informative blog with useful content is not only helpful to your audience, who may then be more likely to buy your products, but it also provides you with a unique opportunity to establish yourself as a leading voice in your field, or an expert in your community. Some blogs have larger readerships than local newspapers, so bloggers can become quite influential and reach a large audience.

Blogs also have a couple of other unique advantages when compared to other forms of social media. First of all, they allow for longer and more in-depth discussions of topics. Whereas on Instagram you could show a photo of a car, on a blog you could post an article discussing in detail the pros and cons of hybrid vehicles. Blogs are ideal for anything that might require a longer format, such as comparison posts, evaluating products or features, solving problems, sharing news and developments, publishing lists, tips, and interviews, and discussing opinions. Blogs can be a great source of information for potential buyers or loyal customers who are seeking greater detail or an extended analysis. That being said, you should take care to organize your posts in a way that is easily readable. Provide clear sections or headlines, avoid extremely long paragraphs, include relevant photos or graphics, and make sure that the format works on mobile devices!

Secondly, blogs are excellent for attracting visitors from search engines, because search engines like new content and fresh content. Blog posts are easy for search engines to index, since posts are usually focused around a specific keyword phrase or search term.

Thirdly, having a blog and adding posts to it over time increases your credibility as a professional, business, and/or thought leader in your industry. Blogging provides a window into your personality, your style, and your way of thinking. Your customers enjoy learning about you and your skillset from what they read on your blog.

And, of course, since social media is never one-sided, blogs provide a great space for community discussion, connection, and feedback. Most blog services have a comments section which can be managed by the owner—you can allow readers to comment freely, or you have the option to review and approve posts and comments before they go live. Ending a blog post with an invitation to readers such as "What do you think?" or "How was your experience with X?" is a best practice for generating discussion and participation. The potential risk is that you may receive criticism or negative comments. These should be addressed quickly and seen as an opportunity to understand the problems and needs of your customers/audience. Negative feedback can certainly help you improve your service or product, and if handled well can improve your image as being responsive to consumers' needs.

Bloggers and commenters alike can include links to other blogs and websites, creating a network of people with shared needs and interests. Make it easy for readers to share the content of your blog across their social networks by adding sharing tools such as the Facebook "like" button or the Twitter "tweet" button to your posts. You can also make it easy for readers to locate your best and most relevant content by including a section such as "best of," "highest rated," or "FAQs."

7.3 FACEBOOK

The importance of Facebook in the world of social media simply cannot be overstated. With more than 1 billion active monthly users, it is the most visited social network in the world and has been described as the "largest media entity in history." In the beginning, Facebook was a site for students to connect with their friends. Today it has become a powerful tool used worldwide for communication, news, business, advertising, organizing, and so much more. Connecting with your target audience and engaging with them through Facebook is a key component of successful social media marketing. Facebook has a variety of features and options suited to different types of businesses (which we'll discuss in more detail below), and the tools and rules of Facebook are constantly changing. However, one thing remains true: On Facebook, like on all social media, the best way to reach your audience is not by creating hype or aggressively selling something, but by creating high-quality content that users will be interested in viewing, reading, and hopefully sharing with their friends. Let's begin by looking at three broad categories on Facebook: personal profiles, groups, and company pages.

Individuals have personal profiles, which can be used to identify yourself, connect with your friends, and share information and interests. It's important to know that using a personal profile for commercial purposes is not allowed on Facebook, and Facebook will shut down an account if they discover that it's being used inappropriately. If you intend to use Facebook for business purposes, you should either create a separate company page (details below) or convert your personal profile to a company page. However, the personal profile can be used in several strategic yet non-commercial ways to support your business.

One option is to add a Follow button to your personal profile. This could be useful if you are a solo enterprise or a figurehead or representative of your company. The Follow button allows your "followers" to see posts that you designate as public, but these followers are not added to your profile as "friends." For example, if you're in business as a personal trainer, you could share personal posts about your favorite movies with friends and family, but also post fitness tips or updates about your schedule and rates to share with your clients/followers.

A similar option is to create custom lists to reach out to specific groups of people among your friends on Facebook. According to the rules of Facebook, these posts cannot be promotional or commercial, but you could share news or events relevant to your industry. If we return to the example of the personal trainer, she could create a list of the people she knows on Facebook who are interested in running and then send those specific people a message about a big marathon that's coming up. Customized lists also help you avoid annoying people with information that is not relevant to them—my friends who are not runners do not have to participate in the conversation about the marathon. But more importantly, it's a great way to open a dialogue, build a relationship, organize an event, or connect with people in a way that could boost your business.

Finally, with a personal profile you can simply inform your friends about your business by posting relevant details or a link to your website or company page in the "work" section of your profile. You can also give your friends a gentle reminder to view your company page with a post

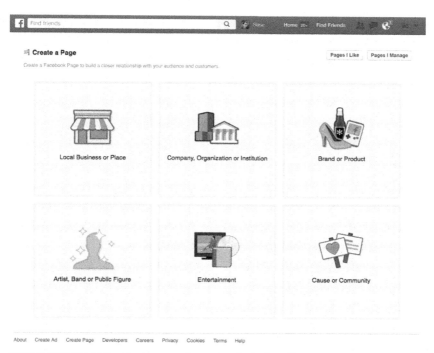

Facebook options for creating a business page. *Source:* www.facebook.com[22]

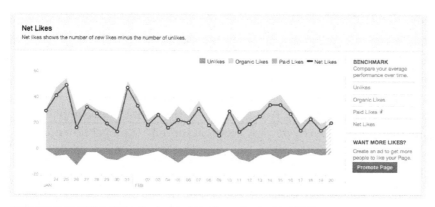

Screenshot of the Netlikes chart in Facebook Insights. *Source:* Facebook Insights[23]

on your personal profile: "Hey everybody! It's been a busy year! Just got my personal training business started. Please check out my page!" Facebook also has a feature called "tagging" which allows you to identify individuals in photos. Not only will the person you tagged see the photo, but their friends will see it as well. Imagine this: the personal trainer posts a photo of six tired but happy runners at the end of the marathon, with the caption "Great job everybody! Thanks for getting ready for the big race with XYZ Fitness." All of the friends of those six tagged people could potentially see that photo. Maybe some of them become interested in your services and contact you on Facebook, or they ask their friends about your company. This generates word-of-mouth promotion, as well as creating a positive social atmosphere by being supportive and encouraging of your friends' and/or clients' achievements.

At the end of the day, Facebook is all about networking, so don't forget that you can use the search feature of Facebook to connect with other people in your line of work, influential leaders, or people with similar interests or needs in your area. You can add them as friends, or send a private message to get a potentially valuable relationship started.

Next, let's talk about company pages, which are also sometimes business pages. A business page is the official representation of a company, but may also be used by other entities such as governments (many cities and countries have Facebook pages for promoting tourism), celebrities and public figures, brands, and nonprofit organizations.

There are a couple of important differences between personal profiles and company pages:

First of all, a company page's connection to the viewer is one-sided. When I "like" a company, I am able to view their public posts and photos, but they are not able to view my personal content. (Compare that to adding an individual as a friend; you would each have access to view each other's profiles.)

Secondly, company pages have a variety of features and useful analytical tools for businesses. For example, in Facebook Insights, you can track the growth of your page, learn which types of posts your audience prefers, get demographic information about your audience, and even keep tabs on your competitors. This information should help you understand your audience and tailor your content to their needs.

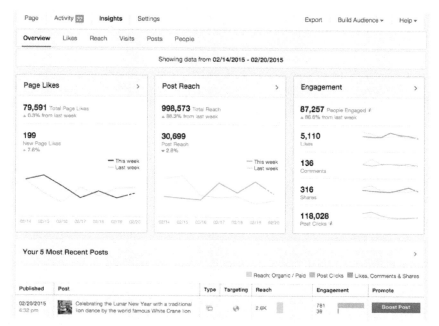

Screenshot of the Insights Dashboard showing Page Likes growth, Post Reach, Engagement data, and the beginning of Your 5 Most Recent Posts. *Source:* Facebook Insights[24]

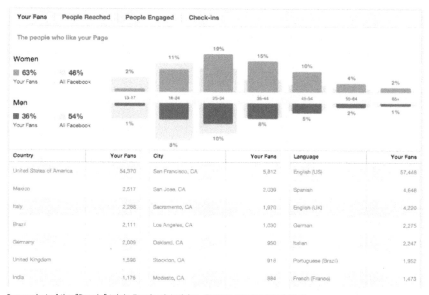

Screenshot of the "People" tab in Facebook Insights. *Source:* Facebook Insights[25]

Advertise on Facebook #19243444 (Susby, USD) ▾

STEP 1: CREATE YOUR CAMPAIGN Use Existing Campaign

Choose the objective for your campaign Help: Choosing an Objective

Boost your posts

Promote your Page

Send people to your website

Increase conversions on your website

Get installs of your app

Increase engagement in your app

Reach people near your business

Raise attendance at your event

Get people to claim your offer

Get video views

Screenshot showing all the various advertising options on Facebook. *Source:* www.facebook.com[26]

Company pages can also pay for advertising in a variety of ways (which is not an option for personal profiles). A "boost" will increase the visibility of your post for a few days. The cost depends on the number of viewers you want your post to reach. A company can also create and pay for a customized advertisement, determining the layout, location, target, and timing. A company can also promote the page in order to get more likes.

In general, when creating a company page, you should follow the same standards you would use in creating any professional material. Choose a good name for your page, and a customized URL can be helpful. A customized URL is also called a vanity URL and you will need to wait until you have at least 30 page likes before you can customize your URL. The cover photo that you use will appear any time you post or your company is liked. This is going to be one of the main images of your company on Facebook, so make sure that you upload a great photo, in the correct format. Provide accurate and up-to-date information about your business, including your address, operating hours, phone number or email, type of business, etc. Providing an accurate description with appropriate keywords will make it much easier for people to find your business in an online search.

There are literally hundreds of ways you can connect with your audience and potential customers via a Facebook company page. You can offer viewers promotions, contests, or special events. Many company pages recognize milestones and achievements, either within the company (post a photo of the employee of the month, or the company's great new location), or those of their customers ("Longtime customer José celebrated his birthday at our restaurant!"). You can encourage customers to "check-in" at your business by using the Places feature. Ask for audience feedback by inviting them to "like" or comment on a photo or post. In fact, a "like" on Facebook has become an important metric for measuring the strength of an advertisement or popularity of a post or item, and the number of "likes" something receives on Facebook is a real indicator of social influence.

Of course, Facebook works together with all of the other forms of social media we'll be discussing, and vice versa. Did the CEO of your company write an excellent blog post? Share it on Facebook! Are there great photos of your newest design on Instagram? Share it on Facebook! And include the Facebook "like" and "share" buttons next to products on your website, interesting articles, blog posts, etc., so that viewers can spread the word as well.

As mentioned above, new features and new rules are constantly being added and updated on Facebook. You'll probably need to research the relevant information for formatting your posts and staying up-to-date with new possibilities as well as legal limitations quite often. Also, remember to monitor your privacy and understand your privacy settings so that you're not caught off guard when Facebook changes something. A good rule of thumb for Facebook, which works for social media in general, is don't do or say anything on social networks or anywhere online that you wouldn't do or say in front of your mother.

Another perspective is to figure out how much time it will take you to maintain your presence on Facebook and engage with your audience in a way that is beneficial to your company. If there is no value in doing this, if it is too much work, or if you don't have the resources to dedicate to it, then Facebook may not be the best platform for you. As Samatha Mykyte points out in her "Should Your Business Say Goodbye to Facebook" blogpost on Wishpond.com,[27] "With so much content being shared, across multiple devices and by billions of people, it's hard to remain competitive and be heard. Do you really expect someone to hear you from across the room at a packed concert? It's the same with Facebook except way, way larger, with way more bands and more people than all the concerts that've happened in the past year.

The algorithm is working and people like it. If Facebook just pumped out the thousands upon thousands of updates from business pages and friends alike, the platform would essentially be Twitter—and we already have that. They've created an algorithm that works for its users."

7.4 GOOGLE+

When it was first launched in 2011, Google+ was considered by many as a potential new alternative to Facebook. With approximately 540 million active users, Google+ cannot compare to the sheer size and dominance of Facebook in terms of popularity. However, Google+ has several interesting features that are not available anywhere else, and this makes it a crucial tool in the online world.

Why use Google+? Have you ever used Google to search for information on the web? If you're like most people your answer will be "every day." Have you ever heard someone say "Just Google it" when they want to find something? Yes. Google searches are so widely used that "to Google" has become a verb synonymous with searching and finding information online. Not to mention Google's other ubiquitous products, including Google News, Google Maps, Gmail, and Google Docs, at least one of which you've probably used at some point. Google basically dominates the field of web searches, and if you want to be found online, you should start by creating a Google+ profile. Building your Google+ profile and circles is a good way to improve your search engine rankings on Google.

While some features of Google+ are superficially similar to Facebook—it's a social networking site where you can connect with friends and post content—there are a couple of key differences. The first difference is the Google+ "Circles." A major drawback of Facebook has always been the difficulty of managing which information you would like to share with your Facebook friends, because on Facebook all kinds of real world friends are lumped in together. Obviously, you don't want to share the same content with all of the different people in your life. (Your college friends want to see your birthday party pictures; you may not want to share those with your boss.) But unless you manage your Facebook account really well, it can be tricky to control who sees what. However, on Google+ users assign their contacts to separate Circles, and can then select which Circles see specific content. For example, a business could create Circles for "VIP customers," "potential clients," and "current partners," sending each of them content tailored to their needs and interests, exclusive offers, or relevant information. On the flip side, you can use Circles to dialogue with people in your industry, or have fans/customers/clients Circle your page on Google+ so that they can stay up-to-date with your developments. An interesting point is that individual members will not be able to see which Circle you have placed them in—the categories you create remain private. Most MBA graduates are well aware of the benefits of market segmentation, and being able to target different audiences with unique information is exactly how Google+ Circles are set up.

The second unique feature of Google+ is Hangouts, which is a way for up to 10 people to join a free video-conference. There are a variety of creative uses for Google Hangouts. Imagine collaborating with colleagues in different cities or countries, or having a convenient consultation with your clients, no matter where they are located. This is a huge asset for any work that benefits from face-to-face communication or requires group discussions. Furthermore, Google Hangouts On Air are automatically recorded and can be posted to YouTube if you choose. You could easily use the Hangouts feature to give a demo, presentation, conference, or workshop, and then share the video on your Google+ profile or other social media. And, as discussed above, because your video is in the Google system it will be easily located by anyone searching for it.

Here's an example of how you could use Google Hangouts if you own a catering company and have been hired for a wedding. Initially, you'll have an online video chat with the clients to discuss their plans and what you can offer. Two weeks later, the bride's brother who is a chef has a lot of suggestions, so you arrange a Google Hangout with the couple, the brother, and yourself to talk it over. No need to go back and forth with a dozen emails; you can talk to all of the relevant parties at once. In the next month, you use Google Hangouts to coordinate with your employees, suppliers and vendors, the wedding planner or event space manager, and nervous family members. Finally, because your customers are so satisfied with your services, they give a brief video testimonial about how great it is to work with you, and you can post this to your Google+ page to show to prospective clients.

So how do you maximize the impact of a Google+ page? You'll need to begin by setting up a business page, not a personal profile. (Like Facebook, these are distinct categories with different functions and uses.) You can get a custom URL which will make it easy for people to find you; once you choose the URL you can't change it, so make sure you pick a good one. Choose a cover photo and profile photo. As with Facebook, make sure the photos are appropriate, attractive, and correctly formatted. Create a tagline, which is a brief summary of what your business is, and complete the "about" section with relevant keywords and links. The more accurately you describe your business, the more likely it is that the right customers will be able to find it in an online search. While Facebook uses "likes," Google uses the "+1" feature to indicate liking, agreement, or support. By adding the +1 button to posts, viewers can easily share your content. Your Google+ page can also be linked to a "Local Places" page if you have a physical location. Local pages include reviews and photos of a business, and can be especially helpful for mobile users who are trying to find you.

In a nutshell, if you want to be found in search results, you should have a Google+ page that is updated periodically with relevant content. Because Google's products are increasingly customized to reflect the users' tastes and preferences, this can really help the right people find you at the right time!

7.5 LINKEDIN

LinkedIn is the world's largest professional social network, with an estimated 200 million users worldwide. It is best used for job seeking and recruitment, retention, industry collaboration, and business-to-business connections. LinkedIn does not have the fun and social atmosphere of Facebook; you will not be using it to share videos of kittens or drunken party pictures. However, it is also very useful. It's a place where professionals can get down to business, so to speak. In fact, some professionals (especially older adults) may feel more comfortable in that environment, and may have a LinkedIn profile even if they do not have a Facebook profile. Therefore, you may be able to reach people on LinkedIn who would not be available through other social media channels. LinkedIn, like Facebook and Google+, allows users to create personal/individual pages, company pages, and groups.

A personal profile functions a bit like an online résumé. In a typical LinkedIn profile, the user will detail their education, experience, and skills. You connect with your friends and colleagues who also have LinkedIn profiles (both parties must approve the connection), and you can then see each other's profile as well as any mutual friends or professional contacts you may share. Your contacts can be organized into groups defined by you, and you can even add notes and reminders for yourself about the contact. You can post and receive recommendations from colleagues and friends. This works a bit like a reference would on a traditional résumé or CV. If your former colleague posts the recommendation "Janet is the smartest and most dedicated person I've ever worked with! She taught me so much." then your prospective contacts or future employer can see the good standing and respect that you have earned in your current or former job. The personal profile also includes a summary, which is a kind of overview statement about who you are as a person and what your professional goals are.

With a personal profile it is also possible to post other media relevant to your work such as presentations, an online portfolio, or a link to a blog post or journal article. Creating a solid profile can certainly help you get a job or a contract, but LinkedIn is not only for those job seekers. If you develop your profile well, providing interesting and informative content,

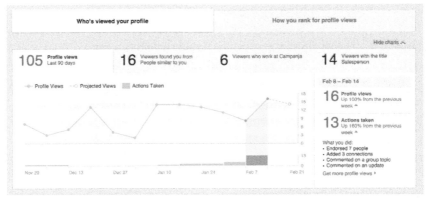

An example of the "Who's viewed your profile" tab on LinkedIn. *Source:* www.linkedin.com[28]

and cultivate your connections with other key players, a great LinkedIn profile can help establish you as a presence—even a leader—in your community or profession. Networking with others in your industry is a powerful asset, whether or not you plan on changing jobs.

Company profiles basically provide an overview of what the business does or what their products are. They often include information about any open positions at the company, and you can also see their employees who are on LinkedIn. A dynamic LinkedIn page is quite useful from a recruitment perspective, as it can draw the most talented people in your industry to seek to work for your company. It's also a great tool for business-to-business connections; this is a space that's much more conducive to professional communication than Facebook.

On LinkedIn it is also possible to create groups for people in your industry to connect and collaborate. If your business is an architecture firm, for example, you might create a group where local architects can discuss new ideas and developments in their field. By using the tools available on LinkedIn, a company can share information, promote events, research their customers' needs, and even get a better understanding of their competition. And LinkedIn company pages are not used solely by for-profit corporations; they are used by entities such as nonprofits and political candidates as well.

LinkedIn also has some interesting new features. LinkedIn Today, now called "Pulse," is a news product launched in 2011. It allows you to

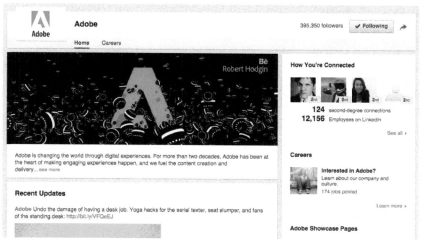

A Showcase page for Adobe on LinkedIn. *Source:* www.linkedin.com[29]

see the articles and stories that are being read most by your contacts and other people in your industry, helping you stay up-to-date with what's going on. Additionally, Showcase Pages were launched in 2013. With a showcase page, you can highlight a specific product, service, assignment, or department. These pages can be followed by users, so it's a good idea to update them periodically with new developments and fresh material.

7.6 TWITTER

Since its launch in 2006, Twitter has attracted 500 million users, 288 million of which are active monthly, and has become a household name. Basically, Twitter is used to post messages consisting of 140 characters or less, which your followers will see. Because of the 140 characters limitation, "tweets" (the name given to these short posts on Twitter) are much shorter than blog posts, and this form of communication is considered more casual than an email. Since the format of tweets is so short, Twitter is often referred to as a microblogging tool. Twitter users can post from any computer or mobile phone, and the "on the go" nature of Twitter is one of the things that makes it unique. Twitter is commonly used to let your followers know where you are, to ask questions, to share opinions, to make complaints, to highlight interesting stuff, and to share links, tips, short videos, and so on.

Because Twitter posts are short, a typical user might tweet three times a day or more, whereas that frequency of activity could be considered annoying on another form of social media. Due to the sheer number of tweets being posted, people who tweet more often throughout the day tend to grow their following more rapidly. Twitter may be the most "in the moment" form of social media, and is often used to share breaking news or to participate in real-time conversations. If you haven't used Twitter yourself, you may have seen a feature on TV news programs that shows viewers real-time tweeted responses scrolling across the bottom of the screen. Likewise, interview programs may invite viewers to tweet their questions and comments, which will then be conveyed to the interviewee then and there.

The basic features of Twitter are as follows: A tweet, as described above, is a general message that goes out to anyone following you. It may consist of text (140 characters or less, of course), an image, a link, or a combination of those. Other users are free to "retweet" a particularly interesting post by someone that they follow. Followers can also use the "favorite" button to show support or approval of a post. The @Reply feature (where you put the @ sign in front of your intended recipient's Twitter handle/ID) lets a user send a message to one or more specific Twitter users; only the recipient and anyone who follows both the sender and the recipient will see it. This feature can help reduce "noise" on Twitter, as users don't need to see a message that does not pertain to them. However, in the event that both the sender and the recipient are high-profile individuals with a lot of contacts in common, their conversation would be seen by a great many viewers. Finally, a direct message (or DM) is a private message between two accounts.

But perhaps the most well-known contribution of Twitter to the world of social media is the use of the hashtag (#). Hashtags are used to group tweets of the same kind together, and can be used by one individual or multiple users. For example, if I'm a parent with a job and several hobbies, I may tweet about a wide variety of topics that I'm interested in. But every time I tweet about my daughter's soccer team I use the hashtag #TemescalTigers. Then, anytime a user wants to see all my tweets that are specifically about the soccer team, they search for that hashtag. Next, all of the other parents, players, coaches, etc., can use the same hashtag, and all of our tweets about the soccer team will be linked together. Hashtags are also useful for conferences where attendees can tweet with the relevant hashtag to indicate to other attendees and non-attendees what they found interesting at the conference. A hashtag for the Search Marketing Expo conference might be #SMX. Recently, hashtags have been especially useful in connecting people with social movements and dialogues. For powerful examples, see #yesallwomen, #blacklivesmatter or #likeagirl. You can see what people all over the world are feeling and saying about current events, or virtually any other topic. The use of hashtags has proven so effective that they have been adopted by other types of social media, and are now used on Facebook and Instagram, among others.

Also remember to check the trends on Twitter, as these show you what is trending at any given moment. Twitter has recently introduced tailored trends, which show you what's trending in topics that you are most likely to be interested in.

Like the social media sites we have already discussed, Twitter can be used by individuals as well as groups, businesses, teams, nonprofits, governments, etc. And of course an individual will use Twitter in an entirely different way than a company will. These days, businesses use Twitter especially to gain insight about their consumers, and it's an important way to get a feel for what the public thinks about your company, products, or service. If you look at the hashtag associated with any major company or brand you'll see a variety of comments, opinions, and feedback about positive and negative experiences posted by customers. Companies can address concerns or bad feedback by tweeting to their followers, or by communicating directly with individuals. Like Facebook, a variety of analytical tools are available to companies for Twitter (http://analytics.twitter.com) so they can measure, for example, how many people clicked on something that they posted, or how many times an item was retweeted.

Businesses can use Twitter in a variety of other ways to interact with the public, promote a product, share information, provide customer service, and network. However, the same rules apply to Twitter as to all other forms of social media: Twitter should not be used as a pushy advertising forum, but rather as a space to provide useful and valuable content. Alerting people who are interested in your brand about special deals or events is acceptable; bulk following, "spamming" people, or hijacking hashtags is not.

7.7 INSTAGRAM

It's an old cliché, but the phrase "a picture is worth a thousand words" could be the perfect way to sum up the value of Instagram. In these days of media overload there is so much content out there that it is literally overwhelming. We can't possibly keep up with the sheer volume of news, data, and chitchat coming at us every day via the Internet, TV, advertising, social media, and on and on and on. The strength of a great photo is that it provides a wealth of information to the viewer without their having to take the time to read something in order to absorb the content. Because we need to take things in at an ever-faster rate, visually oriented media (such as infographics and photos) is on the rise.

The free photo-sharing app Instagram was launched in 2010 and was originally available only on smartphones (iPhone and Android). This was an early indication that the future of social media is in *mobile* media. Instagram has grown to 300 million active monthly users, including everyone from casual shutterbugs to avid photographers. Instagram was acquired by Facebook in 2012 for $1 billion, which gives you some idea of the influence it truly has. One of the beautiful things about Instagram is its simplicity: You take a photo (or a video), apply a filter and add a caption if you wish, and share it on Instagram or other social media. Because of the editing and filtering features, even a beginner photographer can easily transform what was originally a mediocre photo into a pretty cool image. And the serious photography fans can shoot away to their heart's content, sharing their work with the world, or even use Instagram to host a portfolio of their other photographic work.

But Instagram is not merely a site for photographers—it is a social networking site as well. Instagram users connect with their friends, or follow interesting people and companies. Just like Facebook or Twitter, it is a way to keep up-to-date with what is happening and to communicate with the world. Users "like" or "heart" photos, and can leave comments for the photographer. The @ symbol is used to tag specific users, and the hashtag (#) is used—just like on Twitter—to create categories. And Instagram recently added a direct messaging system, so users can share a photo privately with another user, without posting it to all of their followers.

With Instagram, there are also many new ways for businesses to communicate with an audience. Instagram works especially well with industries where you have a beautiful or visually interesting product—fashion, design, travel, restaurants, and the like. However, even if the product itself isn't particularly beautiful, you can bring your brand to life by creating stories told through photos, or by showing happy customers enjoying your brand or services.

One perk of Instagram is that it's quite a fast way to create content. Don't have time or money to arrange a professional photo shoot to market your product? It only takes a few seconds to open the app and snap a photo, and, as mentioned above, you don't need to be a professional photographer to come out with a nice image. Another perk is that there's almost no writing required. You can certainly add an informative or inviting caption if you like, but if you're not a great author or simply don't have time to craft a witty message, the photo alone or accompanied by just a couple of words is totally sufficient. That being said, there is definitely a preference for quality, for artistic well-done photos, over quantity. It's a good idea to pick your one best photo to share, rather than posting ten mediocre images just because you can. And we should not overlook the "insta" part of Instagram. Because it is so quick to take and publish a photo, there's a great sense of spontaneity. You can take a picture with your mobile phone, on the go, and share it right away with the world: "This is what's happening now!" It really is an instant telegram.

Currently, paid advertising on Instagram is limited to just a few companies, but 2015 is the year that Instagram will be offering advertising. But anyone who follows your business on Instagram will see your photos, so there are a lot of options for promoting yourself. One local record shop posts photos of its new arrivals, hashtagging the names of the bands, and in the caption they list prices and store hours, encouraging local customers to come in to the store if they see something they want to buy. Taking that idea a step further, you can advertise special offers, promotions, or flash sales to your Instagram fans. Many businesses post something along the lines of "mention this ad for 10% off today." Instagram contests are also quite popular. A women's clothing line encouraged customers to post photos of themselves wearing something from that shop, hashtagging the name of the shop in the photo, and one contestant won a gift certificate. This, of course, provides great word-of-mouth advertising, as all of the users' friends see these photos, without the company itself pushing anything. For your business, you may of course also share your Instagram photos on your blog and Facebook pages, thus leveraging all platforms. These are just a few of the fun ways that companies have used Instagram; the possibilities are endless.

7.8 PINTEREST

Pinterest can be described as an "online scrapbook" or a "virtual bulletin board" where users can collect and organize images from around the web that interest them. Like Instagram, Pinterest is a very visual app, centered primarily around images. Pinterest's 70 million users (of which 80% are women) can create boards for specific interests, activities, hobbies, or themes. Then when they see an image or bit of content they like (whether on Pinterest itself or somewhere else on the web), they can "pin" it to their board, effectively saving that image or idea. Pinterest's most popular boards tend to focus broadly on fashion, cooking and recipes, interior design, crafts, and gifts, but a user could create a board for just about anything under the sun. Whereas Instagram tends to be photos taken more or less from users' real life, Pinterest boards often reflect people's dreams, wishes, aspirations, and goals. Real boards include themes such as "places I want to visit," "my dream house," and "planning our wedding." As with other social media platforms, Pinterest users connect with their friends or a wider online community, and also follow inspirational people and brands they like. Personal/individual pages are separate from business pages.

So you can probably guess that if your company has a Pinterest page, you can provide images of your products, which your followers can "like" or "pin" to their own pages, sharing them with their own online community. That's great, but it is not the whole story. Pinterest is one of the top five social media sites, and among social media sites it is the second largest driver of web traffic. What does that mean? It means that while Pinterest itself is not a retail site, millions of people end up clicking to check out a website and ultimately buy things that they have seen on Pinterest.

Here's how it works: Your favorite hobby is surfing, so you browse the boards of other surfing enthusiasts. There are a wide variety of boards related to your lifestyle—"best Florida beaches," "Mavericks Surf Competition 2014," "surfing road trip," and so on. On one of those boards you see a great wetsuit—it's just what you have been looking for, and it's recommended by a friend. Based on that image, you have now become interested in a new brand and found an item that you may want to buy. Perhaps you pin that photo of the wetsuit to your own Pinterest board, as a reminder to yourself to check it out later, thereby making it visible to your network as well. Perhaps you find the wetsuit company on Pinterest

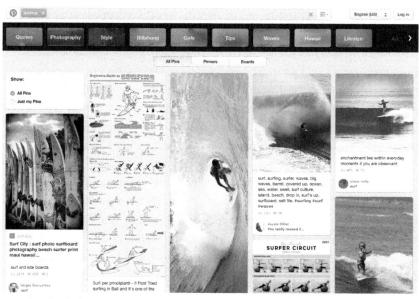

A search for "surfing" on Pinterest reveals a plethora of interesting images about surfing as well as suggestions of other categories to look at above the boards. *Source:* www.pinterest.com[30]

and begin following them, so you can check out their latest products, events, and sales. Or better yet, if you really need that new wetsuit right away, you can click directly from the image to the company's website and purchase it online, or get directions to a retail location. And Pinterest will soon be adding buy buttons, so that people can buy directly from browsing images on Pinterest.

In other words, people don't go to Pinterest specifically to shop, but in the process of exploring their hobbies, lifestyle, and interests they are bound to see images of products they like and that are useful to them. Recognizing this fact, Pinterest has introduced a feature which displays a price tag banner on the picture of a product, making it that much easier for consumers. There are a number of ways that companies can successfully use Pinterest. The first and easiest step is to make sure that your website, blog, or other online content has a "pin it" button, making it easy for anyone who likes what they see to pin your item to their Pinterest board. That goes hand in hand with the concept that you should be sure to provide highly attractive, "pinnable" visual images on your website or other media. You may have a great web store, but if it's mostly text or the pictures are just mediocre, people will likely not be inspired to pin it. Well-designed infographics can be helpful too, if your product or business does not exactly lend itself to being photographed well.

Your company can create its own Pinterest page, which can be used in a variety of ways. The most basic step is to simply show images of your products, which can be pinned and shared by other users. However, to really get the most out of Pinterest you need to remember that it's about appealing to a whole lifestyle. For example, a clothing retailer might have the expected categories/boards of "jeans," "shoes," and "accessories." But to take it a step further, they could create boards such as "date night outfits" or "summer vacation looks." These boards would show not just the product itself, but the product as part of real life. Pinterest can be great for humanizing a company or product as well. Other interesting boards might include themes such as "how it's made," "behind the scenes look," or "meet our team"; these types of boards effectively share the personal story of your brand. Pinterest photos can be humorous, cute, quirky, and unexpected. (If you don't believe me, check out the Pinterest images for

PINTEREST BEST PRACTICES

Edelman Digital

PLAN AHEAD

Be strategic about your brand's Pinterest messaging and concept before launching your brand's page. Think before you pin.

OPTIMIZE YOUR PINTEREST PAGE

This includes linking to your brand's website and Twitter pages and filling out a description. Remember that search engines are indexing your Pinterest boards now so it is important to place traffic-driving keywords in your descriptions and categorize the board correctly.

QUIT TALKING ABOUT YOURSELF ALL THE TIME!

I ♥ ME

As with any social platform, people get bored when brands only share self-serving content. Avoid solely "pinning" self-promotional content as it appears like spam!

PIN WHAT PEOPLE ARE TALKING ABOUT

CROSS PROMOTE, BUT CAREFULLY

Share your pins on Facebook and twitter, but not every single one. Select only the most interesting pins to share on other platforms to avoid over-promotion.

CONNECT WITH YOUR COMMUNITY

Go beyond the repin! Brands should follow, like and comment on other Pinterest users content to maintain a two-way conversation with their audience.

USE BOARDS TO SEGMENT YOUR

An example of an infographic. This one happens to be an infographic about Pinterest. *Source:* www.pinterest.com[31]

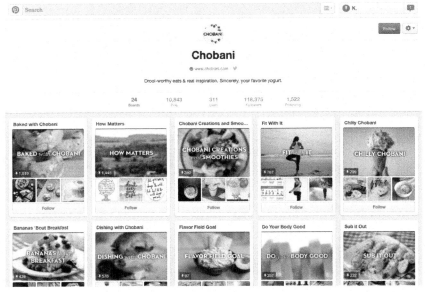

Chobani on Pinterest, showing a variety of Pin Boards. *Source:* www.pinterest.com[32]

Chobani Greek yogurt. Until now, you didn't associate "yogurt" with the words informative, elegant, or fun, did you? Yet somehow their Pinterest photos manage to convey all of that and more.)

Another popular option for companies on Pinterest is to promote special incentives or offers to their followers. Sports brands often offer workout tips, of course packaged as sleek infographics or with attractive images. Food companies offer seasonal recipes. You may ask your followers to participate in a contest, game, or challenge. This can even be a great way to crowdsource photos—your followers will provide great, authentic content. To give one more example: A furniture company could create a special Pinterest board, "Show us your sofa!" Real life customers could pin photos of themselves, their family, and their living room, and tag the furniture company, which could then share their photos on the special board. Other fun ideas include VIP boards, sneak peeks of upcoming products, tutorials and how-to boards, and reviews and recommendations boards. Once again, it is not necessary to focus on selling your product directly, but on getting people interested in your site, brand, or company by offering great content.

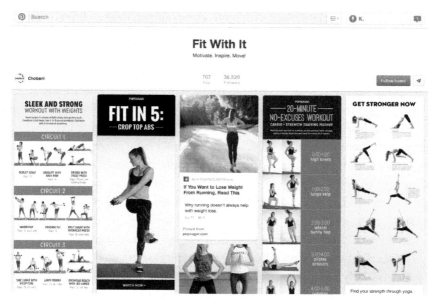

The Chobani Fitness Board on Pinterest. Notice that not all boards are about the product. Some are about fitness, health and sustainability. *Source:* www.pinterest.com[33]

And another way that companies are using Pinterest is to test images. By placing various images on Pinterest and seeing which ones are repinned and favorited the most, businesses can know which image to post on Facebook or Instagram.

7.9 APPS

An app, as defined by http://www.socialfeed.co.za/terms and OxfordDictionary.com, is "a self-contained program or piece of software designed to fulfill a particular purpose, especially as downloaded by a user to a mobile device." These days, there are apps for practically every possible need and want, and new apps are being developed constantly. All of the social media platforms we have discussed so far have an app version, and in fact some of them (such as Instagram and Pinterest) are primarily used on mobile devices, not on desktop computers. Bearing that in mind, it's especially important to make sure that your content is formatted to work correctly with apps. For example, broken links, videos that load too slowly, webpages that are impossible to navigate from a mobile device, or blurry photos are all to be avoided, and will actually annoy your potential customers. Especially if you are hoping to sell anything, the process must be simple, efficient, and work seamlessly.

You may already be familiar with some of the more popular apps. The last year has seen the rise of a variety of transportation apps: Uber, Lyft, and Sidecar are some of them. Car-sharing and rental car companies also typically have their own apps. And many municipalities have transportation apps to help you navigate local systems, and find arrival times, costs, and maps. Aside from Instagram, which we discussed above, there are literally hundreds of apps for taking, editing, storing, and sharing photos. Video apps include YouTube, Vine, and VidStitch, among others.

While it is neither a traditional photography nor a video site, Snapchat is an especially popular image-sharing app, and it reaches a demographic that advertisers are keen to communicate with—young women in their teens and early 20s. Although some features of Snapchat make it difficult to use for marketing, major brands including McDonalds, Audi, Taco Bell, and Mashable have recently started advertising on Snapchat. YouTube also plays brief advertisements before some of its more popular videos. Advertising is possible to a greater or lesser extent in many apps. And of course there are dating apps (Tinder, OkCupid, Match, Grindr, HER), messaging apps (WhatsApp, Viber, HeyTell, Voxer, Line2), travel and tourism apps (Expedia, Orbitz, Flight Tracker, Lonely Planet, TripAdvisor, TripIt), shopping apps, health and fitness apps (Fitbit, Nike Fuelband, Jawbone), cooking apps, news apps, apps for studying and learning, meditation apps (my doctor actually prescribed me the Andrew Johnson sleep app), game apps—literally, there are apps for everything you can imagine. There literally is "an app for that!"

Apps can be "stand-alone" products, or they can also work within or alongside other social media platforms. For example, Facebook is an open platform, which means that anyone can create an application to be used in/with Facebook, which will allow people to share information in different ways. Many of those apps are games, trivia, or quizzes in which players can share their scores, invite friends to play, and compete against each other. A great example of an app that went viral on Facebook was the TripAdvisor "Cities I've Visited" app, which allowed users to pin the cities they have visited on a map displayed on their profile. Without directly selling anything, it was great fun, was shared by many people with their friends, and got a lot of people talking about travel and looking at online travel sites. Other Facebook apps are created specifically for the purpose of E-commerce; they can help you set up a storefront, measure your outcomes on social media, or easily sell products. Some examples are Show & Sell, 8th Bridge (now Fluid), Payvment, Shoutlet, and Shop Tab.

The Cash app allows you to send money to your friends and colleagues from you mobile phone, and all it requires is a phone number or email address.

Finally, if you're feeling overwhelmed by the sheer number of social media sites and apps out there, you will be relieved to know that there are apps developed for the specific purpose of helping you manage your apps. Keeping up-to-date with several different social media sites, as well as producing your own content, responding to friends and customers, and liking and commenting on your followers' posts could easily take up all of your time. For example, an app known as TweetDeck was one of the most popular apps on Twitter. TweetDeck allows users to monitor and tweet from multiple accounts, even allowing users to schedule tweets for delivery at a later time. It also displays Twitter timelines, direct mentions, messages, trends, favorites, search results, and more, all in a customizable display. Another example is HootSuite, which was developed in 2008 specifically for the purpose of managing multiple social media accounts. HootSuite allows users to post messages to many different social media networks, and is useful for managing online brands. Companies as large as Zappos, Martha Stewart Media, HBO, Virgin Group and even the Obama administration are known to use HootSuite to manage their social media interactions. Competitors of HootSuite include TweetDeck, Sprinklr, Nuvi, Buffer, and SalesForceMarketingCloud.

As you can see, there is a truly dazzling number of apps available today. The good news is that most of them are incredibly easy to set up, intuitive to use, and often free or very cheap to download. In many cases, the best way to learn about apps is just to try using them for yourself.

Often, within a few minutes of exploring an app, you'll have a feel for what it does and how to use it.

Do you need your own app? Maybe, and maybe not. Your decision to build one should depend on your goals for the app, and on how often your audience members may use it. Consider the usefulness of an app you are looking to create before you get too far into the app design process. You'll want to make sure that the app is going to be used frequently and not just once per year. For example, if you're a hotel manager, an app to allow guests to book a room and view hotel amenities might not be the best use of your money, since people don't usually book a hotel room more than a few times a year. However, if you approached this by building an app that was geared to offer information about your city and not just your own hotel, the app could be used by your own guests and potential future guests alike. This kind of app would be useful beyond the hotel's core business. That's the kind of app that gets repeat use and could help build goodwill towards your business.

7.10 WHICH ONE IS BEST FOR YOU?

It is probably safe to say that no one form of social media is the "best." Each social media site has its own unique strengths and weaknesses, different functions and drawbacks, its specific audience and niche, and even its own unique culture. Some lend themselves better than others to particular products or services. And your potential customers won't all use the same site, or use social media in the same way. To be most effective in marketing, you'll need to use a combination of different social media sites and approaches to reach customers in the right way. Many companies find that it's best to be active in just a few social networking sites; if you create too many accounts you'll be too busy to be very good at running any of them. The one thing that is certain, though, is that you can't afford to ignore social media—in a recent study, nearly 90% of marketers stated that social media is important for their business and leads to increased exposure for their product. Let's examine the forms of social media we have discussed so far.

Blogs are often considered the "base" or hub of a social media campaign. They are best suited to longer-form articles or extended written pieces. If you'd like to share a full interview or talk about the history of your company, a blog is a great place to do that, so blogs are ideal for raising awareness about your company. This is not to say that blogs are exclusively for text, though; many blogs include photos, graphics, videos, and more. Your fans or customers can reach out to you through a blog as well, posting questions or comments that you can respond to. Blogs work great in combination with other forms of social media too. For example, you could post an amazing photo on Instagram with the caption "For more about my trip to Nepal, check out my blog . . ." and include a link. That way, any of your followers who want more information know exactly where to find it. One thing to keep in mind is that blogs will need to be updated regularly, so you'll need to commit some time to creating and maintaining a blog. Build a calendar and plan out your posts in advance so that you can post regularly and consistently. Remember that blog posts are available for people to find on search engines for much longer than Facebook posts, tweets, or LinkedIn posts, so blogging is a longer-term strategy. Your blog post will have a much longer shelf-life than a Facebook post or tweet.

Facebook, being the biggest social media site out there, has a simply enormous audience and a little bit of everything. It's ideal for increasing your visibility, and allows fans or followers to easily share information about your brand with all their friends. And, like blogs, content from Facebook can easily be shared—either by you or by fans—across other forms of social media. Followers will be regularly reminded about your brand as long as you remember to post updates regularly. Facebook is especially recommended for business-to-consumer communications: Nearly 40% of Facebook users will like a page in order to get a coupon or discount or to participate in a contest, and about 50% of active Facebook users follow at least one brand. Facebook is also good for business-to-business communications because really, as with all social media, it's not building-to-building (business-to-business) but rather person-to-person communication. Facebook is ideal for visually appealing products, as people tend to respond to photos more than text.

Furthermore, Facebook's analytical tools can provide you with powerful insights into your customer base and competition.

In contrast, Google+ is frequently advised for business-to-business brands. For example, Cisco, GE, and HP are major brands using Google+ to interact with and sell to other companies more than to the general public. This may be because Google+ is not as accessible as Facebook. There are more technical things you need to do and understand on Google+ before you can use the tool effectively. Since most of the people on Google+ are still early adopters and "techies," it may be harder to start conversations around other topics. Google+ is crucial to any company that wants to be found easily in a search (search engine optimization), though, or by customers using Google's suite of products. Keep this in mind if you have a physical location! You'll need to make sure that your address and contact information are kept up-to-date, and there are several steps you can take, such as using appropriate keywords, to maximize your visibility in search results. Also, Google+ Hangouts and Circles are unique features that make it easy to organize and communicate with your contacts.

LinkedIn, like Google, is frequently used for business-to-business marketing. In fact, over 90% of business-to-business marketers have a presence on LinkedIn. It is especially known as the most business-oriented of the social media networks. Of course, it is social, in that it's all about connections, but the focus here is on careers, jobs, and business. If you want to network with people in your industry, or establish yourself as a leader in your field, LinkedIn would be the place to start. LinkedIn is also great for keeping up-to-date with what is going on in your field or industry.

Twitter, with its brief format and real-time publication, is ideal for sharing the most up-to-date ideas, trends, comments, news, and developments. If you are in the information or communications sectors, you probably cannot afford to ignore Twitter. It is also increasingly used to provide customer service. However, just because the posts on Twitter are short, you should not underestimate the amount of time you'll need to commit to successfully managing a Twitter account. There are over 27 million tweets per day, so keeping track of tweets about your product or company can be a huge task. Not to mention the need to respond to questions and comments in a timely fashion. Luckily, there are apps like TweetDeck and HootSuite that can help you manage a Twitter account.

You should consider using Instagram if you can regularly produce interesting visual content. This is especially true of some "photogenic" industries such as fashion, design, and travel. You'll need to post often enough to keep viewers interested. Remember that you can post not only photos of your product, but also photos that are relevant to your industry or your fans' lifestyle, and photos that tell a story (for example, "behind the scenes" or "meet the maker" photos). You can also engage your audience by running contests or inviting feedback. Of course, you can link your Instagram account with your other social media platforms.

Pinterest is also a visually oriented site, and like Instagram is especially suited to visually appealing products. However, this does not mean that Pinterest is only for fashion and art. Industries of all kinds have recently found success on Pinterest by using creative visual content. Pinterest is quite often a point of inspiration, leading users to another website, or to making an online purchase (70% of Pinterest users have said they find shopping inspiration there; Pinterest users have the most buyer intent of any of the social networks). Demographically, Pinterest is dominated by women, so Pinterest is a must if you're a brand that caters to women.

You'll need to carefully consider what goals you are trying to achieve with social media marketing, and what is the best way to achieve those goals. Who is your audience, and which are the best sites to reach them? What content is appealing to them? And, on your end, what amount of time and what resources can you devote to maintaining your social media presence? This should help you determine which social media platforms are best suited to the particular needs and resources of your business. One tip: The best way to increase your understanding of social media is to sign up for a personal account yourself and spend some time exploring the sites. Try to understand what the norms, trends, and rules are. What interests you and what annoys you as a consumer? You'll see so many creative ways to engage an audience. Finally, remember that the world of social media is constantly changing. There's always something new, so staying up-to-date with new developments is key.

When you've decided on the sites you're going to use to communicate with your audience, it's a good idea to build a content or editorial calendar, so that you know in advance what you'll be posting in the future and you can find relevant articles, photos, images and videos so that you're not just winging it on a day-to-day basis. This leads us to the next chapter.

CHAPTER 8

CREATING PRIMARY CONTENT

8.1 GENERAL PRINCIPLES: TIMING, FREQUENCY INTERACTION, INTERACTIVITY, TAKING ADVICE FROM YOUR FOLLOWERS, DEVELOPING YOUR VALUE PROP

When you think about the "content" of marketing, is the first thing that comes to mind a print or TV advertisement that tries to convince you to buy a product? This idea is completely outdated and ineffective in the world of social media. Content for social media should not only advertise a product, but also help you get leads about potential customers, get contributions from your fans or followers, or convince people to join your brand, site, or event. There are several general principles that can make your social media more relevant and more effective.

Timing is everything, as the saying goes: Whenever possible, create content that reflects what is going on at the time; if you can, tactfully incorporate current events or trends into your content. For example, if you have a sporting goods store, it goes without saying that you should run images and promotions that reflect the season: baseball gear in the summer, tips for skiers in the winter, and an interview with a soccer coach when the World Cup is happening.

At the very minimum, you need to make sure that your content is not old, stale, and out of date. When using social media, you should also be mindful of the timing of your posts. You'll need to post frequently enough to keep your audience interested, but not so often that you annoy them. The frequency at which you post should vary with the type of media you use. You may also notice more or less impact from your content depending on the time of day you post. Some recommend posting in the morning and evening, when people are most likely to be browsing social media. Others recommend posting at odd hours like late at night when there will be less competition and your message can really stand out. Try posting at different times and see what reactions you get!

Recommended frequency of posting by platform:

BLOG	RECOMMENDED FREQUENCY
FACEBOOK	1 × PER DAY
GOOGLE+	3× PER DAY
PINTEREST	3× PER DAY OR AS MANY TIMES AS POSSIBLE
INSTAGRAM	1 × TO 2× PER DAY
TWITTER	22 × PER DAY
YOUTUBE	1 × PER WEEK OR 1 × PER MONTH

Interaction among contacts, friends, and companies is the heart and soul of social media, and what sets it apart from old-fashioned advertising. Look for ways to facilitate and encourage interaction when posting content. A forum or discussion page can be a great way to involve potential customers in a community of people who use your product. Ask questions and start discussions. Or, get your existing customers to interact with each other by organizing an event, either online or in the real world.

Making your content interactive is a great way to ensure that your site is engaging and dynamic. Many sites feature tools or activities that get the visitor to participate in an action. For example, many political websites include an "email your senator" feature. Others include games or quizzes that are personalized to the user.

Remember that this conversation goes two ways; social media provides you with a great opportunity to really listen to your customers and fans. Make sure that they can easily find the information to contact your business or office. Provide them with opportunities to like, rate, review, or leave comments. But don't stop there—take action on the feedback that you receive. If a customer posts a question, that could be a great inspiration for a blog post. If you notice a lot of feedback requesting something, see if you can make it happen! Remember the mantra: "What's in it for them?" In other words, build content around topics that are interesting and useful to your audience.

Last but not least, quality content posted on social media should help position you as an expert in your field, or establish your brand as a trusted and respected company worthy of loyalty. A great way to do this is by demonstrating your passion and expertise about a given topic. Being recognized as a knowledgeable thought leader will add value and credibility to your brand.

8.2 WHAT'S THE BEST TYPE OF CONTENT TO POST ON SOCIAL MEDIA?

Naturally, the best type of content to post varies with the social media platform. Remember that there is quite a bit of overlap between the different platforms (e.g., a photo that is posted on Instagram may also be pinned on Pinterest). However, there are some broad trends that can help you tailor your content to match the interests of different audiences.

Take a look at some of the data from 2014: On Facebook, the most frequently shared content tended to be quizzes, heartwarming or motivational stories, and entertainment news. On Twitter, the most shared tweets were breaking news, business articles, and stories that spread awareness. LinkedIn was, of course, dominated by industry news items, especially in the fields of technology, environment, and real estate. Pinterest posts focused on fashion, DIY projects, and recipes. And the

Best in class brands to emulate by platform. *Source:* www.digitalinformationworld.com[34]

most-shared items on Google+ were celebrity news, sports articles, and deals and coupons.

This definitely does *not* mean that you should limit yourself to posting content according to these trends. It's more of a general guideline for what audiences have come to expect and often respond to on the various sites. If you follow the general principles discussed above regarding timing, interactivity, and feedback, you should be well on your way to producing dynamic content that goes over big on any social media platform.

A further tip is to create content with "pass-along value." Why do people share content with their online networks? Because it is intriguing, useful, important, entertaining, or just plain crazy! There are many ways to create content that viewers will want to share, and directly pushing your product is possibly the least advisable among them. Try posting what is known as "adjacent content"—something that is related to the interests and lifestyle of your audience. As described above, a sporting goods store could share a particularly inspiring interview with a famous athlete. This type of content is relevant to your audience, so they will want to share it with their own friends and family. Another option is to post useful advice, tips, tricks, or how-tos that will help your viewers solve a common dilemma or use your product in a better way. Or share stories about what makes your company unique. Do your employees do volunteer work? Have you recently achieved something amazing? Don't be afraid to share good news from behind the scenes. This helps personalize your company. And finally, be funny! Everyone loves to laugh. (Although you need to carefully consider the specific content before you post—not everybody finds the same things funny. Avoid offensive or derogatory humor.)

Predicting what people will enjoy and share is not an exact science, but the best content will be shared (pinned, retweeted, liked, linked, blogged) by hundreds, possibly thousands, of viewers. And if you're really lucky, it could even go viral! Look at what happened with the ALS Ice Bucket Challenge. See www.alsa.org/fight-als/ice-bucket-challenge.html to learn how they were able to achieve more donations than they have ever received before. Just through this one social media campaign, they raised $115 million for ALS. People challenged each other on Facebook and Twitter to take the Ice Bucket Challenge, and with each challenge accepted, ALS received more and more awareness and the donations kept pouring in.

TAKING THE CHALLENGE.............................

- When doing the challenge, please use the hashtags #icebucketchallenge, #alsicebucketchallenge, and #strikeoutals.
- The Ice Bucket Challenge may not be suitable for small children, the elderly, anyone in poor health or animals of any kind, so please use good judgment.
- Please be thoughtful about water usage. If you're in an area of the country or world affected by drought, please consider making a donation instead, or repurpose the water for later use.

ALS Ice Bucket Challenge guidelines. *Source:* ALS Association[35]

Thank You for the outpouring of support.
Since July 29, 2014, The ALS Association has received **$115 million** in donations!

The power of social media when something goes viral; results of the ALS Ice Bucket Challenge. *Source:* ALS Association[36]

The quality of the content that you post can and should go far beyond mere advertising. By posting great quality content you have a chance to improve the reputation of your company, become a trusted brand, establish yourself as a thought leader in your industry, and set yourself apart from your competitors.

8.3 TEXT

With all this variety of social media platforms available, there are a lot of different writing formats out there: blogs, press releases, white papers, email newsletters, comparison pieces, e-books, interviews, tweets, etc. Each has its own use and requirements; however, here are some guidelines for better writing, no matter what the format is.

The first and possibly most important rule is to write for a specific audience and focus on solving the problems of your buyer in language that they understand. All too often, marketing departments produce writing that sounds vaguely impressive but completely fails to speak to your actual customers. You should think carefully about exactly who your audience is, what their problems or needs are, and how your product can help them. Some PR experts recommend creating what is called a "buyer persona," or brand hero. A buyer persona/brand hero is basically a fictional profile of someone representative of your actual customer base. It is based on market research, demographics, and data about your clients. But you'll add details to the profile that will help you think about your customers in a more human way, understanding what their more general needs and goals are as well as what they buy and why. For example, a buyer persona for a client of the sporting goods store could be "Teenager Brad." He's a varsity football player, between the ages of 14 and 18. Because he's a student he has limited income. What are his other hobbies? Another buyer persona could be "Janet," who's a retired mom dealing with health problems. Her interests are yoga and walking. Her income and shopping habits are totally different from Brad's. Now, in real life you probably would not speak to these two different customers in the same way, right? You might change your tone, your vocabulary, even the topic of your conversation, to reflect their needs and interests. While of course it's impossible to specifically target every single member of your audience in your writing, conducting a thought experiment like creating a buyer persona should really help you focus on *who* you are trying to communicate with, what you have to offer them, and what is the best language to use to reach them. Think about writing from the perspective of your buyer, not your marketing department.

Use a simple template like this one to create your buyer persona/brand hero.

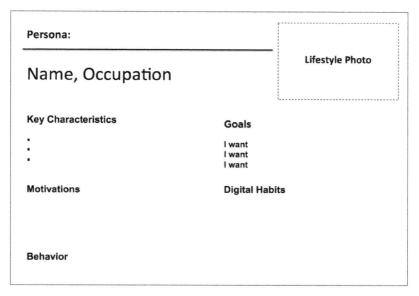

A simple template for creating your buyer persona/brand hero. *Source:* www.sharpspring.com[37]

Now that you've identified who you are writing for and what their needs and interests are, there are a couple of common pitfalls you should be sure to avoid: industry jargon, clichés, and meaningless junk! Some words and phrases are so overused that they have become just more annoying nonsense, which will quickly bore your audience. Some good examples of phrases to use with caution are: *world-class, industry standard, unparalleled, market leader, cutting-edge,* and *next generation.* You've probably heard these phrases in everything from car commercials to toothpaste ads. A good hint is that if the language you are using to describe your product could be used just as easily for just about any other product, you may not be writing effectively, and you are certainly not setting your company apart from your competition. And don't be afraid to get feedback about your writing. For example, if you write a blog post and then receive comments such as "What does it mean?" or "You used the word *solution* fifteen times in one paragraph" then you have just received some valuable help in improving your writing.

So, as we discussed above, the first step in good writing is to identify your audience, and the next step is to identify your goals and the appropriate venue. What is it that you are trying to communicate in your writing? The possibilities here are endless: Telling your customers about a new product? A milestone in your company? A solution to a problem? An award that you won? A heartwarming story about your employees? Look for opportunities to share relevant and interesting stories with your audience.

Once you have determined your audience and your goal, you should consider what style of writing is most appropriate and what is the best social media platform to share it. Breaking news might be best suited to Twitter, while a quiz about the history of bicycles could be more fun on Facebook.

But you don't have to be limited to just one social media platform. Remember that you can, and should, share content across multiple platforms. Make it easy for your followers to identify and re-share by adding any appropriate links, tags, hashtags, "like" or "pin" buttons, and so on. Choose a great title that will catch people's attention. And make sure your content is easily found by people who may be searching for it by using appropriate keywords. These steps will help you maximize the impact of your content.

Finally, as mentioned in Part I, identify the author or source of the writing, especially if you are posting in a forum where the source could be unclear. For example, in many companies multiple people have access to the company Twitter account. Whoever posts should sign off with their initials so that there is accountability. This can also help personalize your writing. It can be interesting for your audience to hear from different members of your team, with their different perspectives, rather than you coming across as a monolithic organization.

8.4 IMAGES

Images are the most popular and most shared content on social media sites. When we discuss images, this is not only limited to photos; images include cartoons, drawings, charts, graphs, infographics, screenshots from videos, and so on. And social media images are more likely to be considered in a positive light than text posts. If a typical user has a complaint to make, they'll likely explain via a written post on Twitter or Facebook, whereas it's a bit more difficult to post an image for "complaint." Furthermore, brand promotion by means of photos or other images is often perceived more favorably than written promotion. Seeing a photo of a cute sweater posted by a retailer strikes customers as less obnoxious than reading the statement "Our sweaters are the cutest so buy one today." Right? Logically, carefully considering your images and visual content needs to be a major focus of your social media strategy.

If done well, that photo of the cute sweater, or whatever image you choose to use, will not come across as "advertising" or "marketing." One thing to be aware of is that generic stock photos are pretty unappealing. Customers can usually tell when a stock photo is used because such photos simply have a fake look, and this can have a negative impact on your campaign or brand. Shooting your own photos or creating your own graphics is strongly recommended, as this will convey a more authentic feeling. Realistically, depending on your time and budget constraints, it can be pretty difficult to produce 100% of your own visual content. There are many online sources for finding or editing stock photos, but these should be used selectively.

Having taken the time and effort to create great visual content, you want the credit for it, right? With any luck, after you post a photo it will be liked, shared, reposted, and in other ways passed around the web by followers and fans. The photo will travel from your company's own social network or website where it was originally posted to other networks, platforms, and websites. So how will anyone know that it's *your* image? This is where branding comes in, to make sure your fans can effectively recognize your visual content wherever it ultimately appears. One way to do this is to add an unobtrusive logo, website address, or twitter handle to the image. Another, more subtle way, would be to use a consistent

King Oscar Seafood
February 20 ·

WIN AT THE OSCARS WITH KING OSCAR!!!
Simply comment here with your vote for Best Picture, Best Actor, and Best Actress by 2pm PT Sunday Feb 22. Get them all right and you could take home a [King] Oscar! We're talking coupons, beer openers, t-shirts, aprons or other fun prizes in a random drawing! It's #Oscars Night!

AND THE [KING] OSCAR GOES TO...

Like · Comment · Share · 142 55 5

An example of a post on the King Oscar Seafood Facebook page. *Source:* www.facebook.com[38]

King Oscar Seafood
February 14 ·

SHOW YOUR BODY & YOUR TASTE BUDS A LITTLE LOVE...
Eat some delicious, nutritious fish! Better still, share your favorite seafood recipe here today and tomorrow for a chance to win a free KO coupon. HAPPY VALENTINE'S DAY FROM KING OSCAR!

Like · Comment · Share · 261 28 20

Notice that all posts have red in them and often show the product in it's packaging in creative ways. *Source:* www.facebook.com[39]

format or uniform template (colors, fonts, filters, frames, etc.) which will represent your brand.

King Oscar Seafood does a great job of this on Facebook. Their images usually have the King Oscar red in the background and/or the logo or product in them. Their images are mostly original and witty.[40] See www.facebook.com/KingOscarSeafood for more.

There are some instances where you will not want to use a logo or brand in an obvious way on your photo. For example, if you plan to post some content for the anniversary of 9/11, slapping your big corporate logo onto an image can come across as crass and disrespectful. In some cases, fans may also be more likely to share and repost an image *without* a visible brand, because it seems more personal and less corporate. If you find that posting images without a visible brand gets you more shares, you could consider a built-in attribution such as a link to your website that will accompany the image every time it is reposted. That way, when someone comes across the photo of the cute sweater on their friend's Pinterest board dedicated to fall fashion, they can easily trace the photo back to the original source—your website or store.

Overall, the most effective images require little to no extra explanation. They should be eye-catching, entertaining, intriguing, or emotional on their own. In fact, in many cases the image does not even need to show a scene that is related to your brand directly, as long as it portrays the feelings you want associated with your brand. A strong image will speak for itself. Inspirational and motivational images, often accompanied by quotes, tend to perform especially well on social media, as they trigger an emotional response. Similarly, nostalgic or historical images that evoke the past are highly shareable, and so are images of beautiful natural scenery, and of course funny images.

There are numerous creative ways to use images in your social media marketing. The first, and most obvious, is to run an ad, incentive, promotion, or special offer by means of a catchy photo and accompanying text. However, photos of your actual customers (whether taken by you or submitted by them) can be a more powerful form of testimonial. Encourage your audience to post their own photos, tagging you or mentioning you in the post. Then you can collect and share these photos using a hashtag or special album. Also, remember that customers who are looking at your product online can't examine an item like they would in real life, so you may want to use images to highlight features or functions that they may not be aware of otherwise. If there are technical details, data, statistics, or facts that you would like to share, consider creating an eye-catching infographic or chart, rather than just writing a list of numbers. Similarly, word clouds, screenshots, and slides can bring otherwise boring data to life by effectively using fonts, colors, and layout to create a pleasant and appealing image.

Finally, don't be afraid to experiment with trends in popular culture. Photobombing and selfies are two photo fads that have probably transcended the "trend" label and have now become permanent fixtures in our cultural and visual landscape. Similarly, humorous memes (discussed in more detail in chapter 11) may come and go quickly, but they can be a funny and generally harmless way to connect with your audience.

8.5 VIDEOS

Video and audio clips became much more popular with the advent of sites such as YouTube, Vimeo, Vine, and iTunes and the widespread availability of high-speed internet. Not only that, but with the current generation of smartphones, almost everyone has the ability to easily create, upload, and share videos with the world, and videos can easily be watched on-the-go or shared with friends. YouTube, in particular, is simply massive. It is the world's largest video-sharing site with over one billion users. In fact, it's difficult to even say how many videos are currently on YouTube because more than 300 hundred hours of video are uploaded to the site *every minute*!

You might think that YouTube (not to mention the other video hosting sites) is so huge that your video will be lost among the billions of videos available. But one thing to keep in mind is that YouTube—which, incidentally, is owned by Google—is the world's second largest search engine. That means that people actively turn to YouTube to search for information and find out about things that they want to know. For this reason, it's a great idea to consider making videos that answer your customers' questions, for example a how-to, a tutorial, or a video that shares your expertise. True story: I once googled "how to open a pomegranate" and ended up on YouTube, because that's precisely the kind of information that's easier to absorb by watching than by reading step-by-step instructions. The YouTube video that I watched was made by POM Wonderful, a company that makes—you guessed it—pomegranate juice. That video did not lead me to purchase anything that day, but it did help me open a pomegranate, and I thought it was pretty cool that POM Wonderful had made that handy video. To maximize the likelihood of your video being found in a search, make sure to give it a good title, and use relevant keywords in the description or "about" section.

As you can see from the pomegranate example, some material is just easier to show in video format than by writing. This can come in handy for product demos or reviews as well. A demo, and even more so a review, does not necessarily have to be produced by your company. If there are fans out there who have made their own videos using or reviewing your product, those can be useful too. In fact, customer-generated videos can be more authentic and convincing than content produced by your company.

Another advantage of videos is that, compared to writing, it can be easier to express your personality and sense of humor through them. For example, you may want to interview experts, introduce viewers to members of your staff, or show a motivational speech made by one of your executives. In that case, try to have the people in your video appear as relaxed and natural as possible. They don't need to be professional actors by any means, but try to make sure they don't come across as too nervous, stiff, or awkward. When possible, select people that are at ease on camera to appear in your videos. These "slice of life" videos can go a long way toward humanizing your organization.

Just as YouTube viewers do not expect professional actors, they also do not expect professional, Hollywood-level production values. In most cases, videos will be quite short (often 2 minutes or less) and can even be shot on a smart phone or flip camera. Obviously, a video that looks and sounds terrible will reflect poorly on your business, so you should take care that there is adequate lighting and that the camera angles show things clearly. If you plan on using videos extensively, you may want to invest in some basic editing equipment, lighting, or microphones, but for many companies that won't be necessary. And in most cases, it is really the content more than the production value that matters.

As mentioned, many videos—especially instructional ones—are very short, just one or two minutes. You'll need to get to the point, delivering the content up front. If people feel that their time is being wasted, they'll simply stop watching. Of course, some types of videos may run longer than a few minutes, depending on the topic and material; but keep it enjoyable as much as possible.

Targeting young men, DollarShaveClub.com (with owner Michael Dubin starring as himself) was able to break into the very competitive $13 billion razor blade industry with this short video. The video was so successful that the company had 12,000 customers the second day after the launch of the website. Go to www.youtube.com/watch?v=ZUG9qYT JMsI to watch the video.

Aside from the examples discussed above, there are many other fun approaches to creating a YouTube video. Just about anything that

DollarShaveClub.com - Our Blades Are F***ing Great

Dollar Shave Club ☑

▶ Subscribe

18,635,341

➕ Add to   ＜ Share   ••• More

👍 101,873   👎 1,794

The video that took down the servers due to too many visits when Dollar Shave Club launched in 2012.
Source: www.youtube.com[41]

you could produce in a written format could also be done by video (for example, news, announcements, sharing opinions, press releases, etc.). However, in videos perhaps more than other formats the content is expected to be entertaining; make it clever, unexpected, and don't make it feel like a marketing pitch.

Although we have mainly discussed YouTube here, videos can be shared across most of the social media platforms, so don't forget to provide links and "like" and "share" buttons. And just like in other forms of social media, you need to be responsive to comments, complaints, and questions from your audience. Whenever possible, make it interactive by inviting your audience to share their own videos, or by running a special contest or event.

8.6 PODCASTS

Podcasts are audio content that listeners can subscribe to, receiving regularly updated segments and listening to them at their convenience. While the content may be similar to an old-fashioned radio show, listeners get to choose exactly what they want to listen to; you can find a podcast for any niche interest. And because the podcast is downloaded to your device (computer, iPod, or smartphone), you can listen anytime and anywhere you choose. Millions of people enjoy listening to their favorite podcasts while they're commuting, working out, or just relaxing at home. And while radio stations are finite and local, podcasts are limitless and worldwide.

Podcasts, like blogging or video, can be a great source of the kind of consistent, rich content that you will need to produce if you want to maintain a social media presence. The basic principles of creating a dynamic podcast are the same as for a blog or video: Consider your specific audience and create thoughtful content that addresses their interests, needs, or problems. Ideally, you will be speaking about something that you (and your guests) are passionate about, and you will have something special to bring to the table; perhaps a perspective that your guests won't hear anywhere else. Even if it's a topic that you love to talk about, preparation is especially important in podcasting, because you'll want the program to flow smoothly. While some speakers may perform well speaking off the top of their head, most will prefer to have a script or an outline prepared. This also helps keep your topic focused and ensures you have all the relevant information at hand when you need it.

Compared with other forms of social media, podcasting requires a bit more effort, know-how, and equipment. The equipment that you'll need to start podcasting ranges in cost from a few hundred dollars to over a thousand for professional-grade sound. It's probably a good idea to do a few podcasts and see if it works for you before investing in expensive gear. You will also need to pay to host your audio files on an external server. You can record directly onto your computer using a microphone and software such as Audacity, GarageBand, or ProTools, but if you plan on recording "in the field," perhaps at various events or locations, you will need mobile recording gear. You could also use a digital recorder to record conversations that are held via Skype or Google Hangouts. You can upload the audio files as you recorded them if you are satisfied with the results, or you may want to clean up the sound quality and content using editing software. (Conveniently, you can use Audacity, GarageBand, or ProTools for editing as well as recording sound.)

After you've recorded, edited, and uploaded your podcast, it is essential to tag the audio so that people can find what you've made. Because this is an audio file, you have to add text-based information and accurate keywords, so that when people search for a relevant topic online, your content will come up. Similarly, many podcasters produce a companion blog which discusses the content of their show, or even includes a full or partial transcript. You may even want to include time codes, to help listeners locate exactly the content that they want in the audio files. Again, this will increase the chances that your content will be easily found in an online search. A companion blog is also a great way to provide links to the blogs or websites of your guests, company, or other relevant sites.

Then you need to host (there will probably be a monthly fee for hosting) and distribute the audio files to the public via a network such as iTunes. Last but not least, let everybody know about your podcast so they can tune in! Put links to your podcast on your other social media, and mention it in interviews. Often, guests who are featured on your show will help you promote it too.

CHAPTER 9

MANAGING SECONDARY CONTENT

9.1 FEEDBACK

The uses of social media go far beyond the updates and images you will post to reach out to your audience. It is often said that in a good conversation, you should spend about 50% of the time listening—and this means *actively* listening, paying attention and carefully considering what the other person is saying, not just waiting for your turn to speak. This rule also holds true in the world of social media and marketing. Social media provides you with an invaluable opportunity to listen and get honest feedback from your customers and clients. And don't think of feedback as merely complaints or criticism; feedback is the positive input that you'll need to improve your product and advance the goals and objectives of your business. You should incorporate feedback at all points in the cycle of your product or service, from asking your customers to help determine what new products you should develop, to customer reviews after the product is sold.

The first step, of course, is to connect with your audience on social media, and provide lots of clear ways for them to give you feedback. Make sure that your contact information is easy to find, and that your customer service department is accessible. This may include changing the way your customer service department works, as you'll need to make sure that the right people have access to social media accounts, and are trained in appropriate ways to respond. (Having a clear social media policy for your staff and employees is recommended, whether they are in customer service or another department.) You'll need to not only set up the avenues for feedback and complaints, but actively monitor them as well. These days, customers expect prompt responses to online complaints or problems, so even if you don't have an immediate solution to offer, you should at least acknowledge the post and let them know that you are working on it. Especially on social media, one of the worst things you can do is leave negative feedback unanswered. Because a complaint is potentially seen by many other people, you will appear unresponsive and unconcerned about the needs of your customers. On the other hand, don't hesitate to share positive feedback with the appropriate people in your company, or even with your online community. It's a great way to boost morale and generate good cheer.

Add buttons for customers to like, share, retweet, or pin items. This is, after all, one way of measuring approval. You can easily see which items get the most responses. And if a blog post or photo receives zero likes, no comments, or generates no interest, then maybe it was a bad idea? In that case, you know that you'll need to refine your ideas or improve your content.

Feedback from your customers and fans should play a big part in helping you develop new ideas and products. You should be taking notes of what your customers want and need; which new features would be most useful for them? You can use social media to convene a focus group, or invite members of the public to "test drive" a new product. This can be especially productive if you invite bloggers, podcasters, journalists, or experts in your industry to try something out. Their feedback will be useful to you, and they are also likely to share their experiences and comments with their own networks as well.

Finally, follow up! Get feedback and customer reviews after the sale. Many websites invite customers to take a quick survey or poll at the end of their transaction, or a few days later. For example, Amazon typically sends an email after a product has been delivered, asking the customer if they are satisfied with the product, delivery time, and service, and inviting them to post an online review. These reviews are a powerful tool in helping others decide what to buy, but also in helping Amazon to improve its service.

Last but not least, you should monitor conversations and feedback from around the web. This is an important way to keep in touch with what the public is saying about your company, your industry, similar products, and even your competitors. For example, if your competitor receives a lot of negative feedback, you've just learned what to avoid doing.

How do you monitor conversations and mentions of your brand? There are several tools for this, some of them free and some available on a monthly subscription basis. If you need a free tool, try SocialMention.com or Mention.com and Google Alerts. If you have a budget for a more robust tool and platform, which can monitor tens of thousands of mentions across several clients, competitors, or industries, then try Nuvi, SalesForceMarketingCloud.com, or Sprinklr.

9.2 RESPONSES/COMMENTS

As we learned in our discussion about feedback, in the world of social media it is critical to monitor and respond to everything as much as possible. That includes the responses that the public will make to things that you post, as well as comments that they will make either on your site or on other sites in a discussion about you. While some companies hesitate to get involved in social media for fear of the negative comments and responses they might get, this is not actually a situation to be avoided as long as you have a solid plan for how to handle complaints. In fact, handling adversity well should serve to boost trust in your competence as an organization and increase goodwill.

If you're really concerned about negative comments, there are a few things you can do to prevent them before they happen. Make it as easy as possible for people to solve problems for themselves online, or to contact you directly to solve a problem, by creating a FAQ section as well as easy access to email, private message, or appropriate phone numbers. Also, if there's some not-so-positive news about your company, you can use your social media profile as a way to break the news yourself, publish a response, and show that you are taking responsibility and action.

Domino's Pizza did this when the CEO of the company made a public video response about a scandalous video prank produced by former employees who described how they contaminated the food.

Dirty Dirty Dominos pizza

Ramox3's channel

Subscribe 266

1,262,228

+ Add to   < Share   ••• More   👍 831   👎 312

The Dirty Domino's Pizza Crisis in 2009. *Source:* www.youtube.com[42]

Domino's President Responds To Prank Video

swifttallon's channel

Subscribe 402

158,494

+ Add to   < Share   ••• More   👍 264   👎 51

The President of Dominos Pizza's response to the Dirty Dominos incident.
Source: www.youtube.com[43]

McDonald's Canada has a page where customers can ask questions, and often they respond with video answers. See http://yourquestions .mcdonalds.ca/.

When you do receive negative comments, the two biggest rules of thumb are Don't ignore it, and Don't delete it. You should respond to negative comments as quickly as possible. Not responding sends the message that you simply don't care about your customers and their problems. Some top companies try to respond in one hour or less; if this is not an attainable goal, even responding within 24 hours is better than nothing, and there are many apps and programs that can help you keep track of mentions of your company. Often, a simple apology or offer to communicate further in private can defuse the situation, as most customers just want to be heard and treated like a human. And, in the case of a positive comment, a simple "thanks" or "like" is all that's needed.

However, you should never delete a legitimate complaint or criticism. This tends to make the complaining customer even more angry, and casts you in a negative light with your other fans as well. You should absolutely be aware that in the age of social media, hitting "delete" does *not* make something disappear. Too many people will have already seen it and potentially taken a screenshot or in some other way saved the negative content. The only way forward is to deal with it honestly and responsibly.

There is one important exception to the "do not delete" rule, and that is content that is truly offensive—for example, racist, sexually explicit, profanity-laden, threatening, malicious, or violent comments. At least on your own social media pages, you can and should post guidelines about what content is allowed, and then monitor carefully, removing offensive comments if necessary. This keeps the online community a welcoming place for everyone, and a place where legitimate complaints are acceptable. You may find it helpful to post guidelines such as the following: *"We appreciate your interest in our page and thank you for leaving comments, photos, videos, and links here. However, we do review all comments and will remove any that are offensive or inappropriate. Thanks for your participation."* In extreme cases, it may even be necessary to document the offensive comment, delete if from the page, and block or report the commenter to the proper authorities.

Here's a little case study. If a customer posts a neutral comment ("I'm staying at XYZ hotel"), you may not even need to respond. If they post a positive comment ("I'm staying at XYZ hotel and the staff are so friendly!"), you could respond with a "like," or "Thanks! We appreciate your business." If they post a negative comment about a real problem ("I'm staying at XYZ hotel and my room is filthy! Yuck!"), then you need to respond as soon as possible with an appropriate remedy—for example, "We're very sorry you've had a problem. Please contact the front desk . . . " Or perhaps you could upgrade them to a nicer room. However, if they post a negative comment that is offensive, irrational, and violates your rules ("I hate this hotel, Joe is a **** and I'm going to burn it down!"), go ahead and save a copy, delete it (explaining why), and alert the authorities if you feel it's necessary.

9.3 SURVEYS

Surveys, questionnaires, and online polls can be excellent tools for conducting market research and getting more information about the opinions, wants, and needs of your online followers. Surveys can also help you evaluate the success of your programs in a budget-friendly way. As in any research venture, the first step is to identify exactly what you need to know and who you should be asking. Define the target audience for your survey, and then choose the appropriate social media channels to best reach them. You should also take into consideration if your target audience is likely to be using social media and responding to your survey on a mobile device or desktop computer, on the go or at home, as this will determine how much time and attention they devote to answering your survey, as well as what format is most suitable.

There are many online tools that offer readymade survey templates or can help you create customized surveys, such as Survey Monkey, Survey Gizmo, 4Q Survey, and Kwik Survey, to name but a few. Some of them have a basic, free option, which is great for short, informal surveys, as well as a more elaborate version with greater flexibility, that you would have to pay for. You'll need to evaluate the tools that are available in each survey program in order to find one that matches the scope of your research and meets your analysis needs. One thing to consider is if you

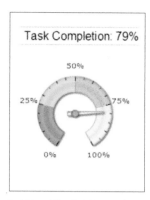

Task Completion Rate is a good source for how well customers are able to complete certain tasks. A survey is the only way to find this information. Photo Credit: Avinash Kaushik *Source:* www.kaushik.net[44]

need to customize the look of the survey, choosing your own fonts, colors, graphics, and so on. Other features that you may or may not need include "skip logic," which allows the reader to skip ahead if they answer "no" to a particular question, "piping," which produces a specific question on the basis of the previous answer, and "randomization," which puts the questions in random order. Finally, when choosing a survey tool you should consider what kind of data analysis (reports, summaries, statistical analysis) is available with the package.

You can invite people to take your survey by sending them an email link or by posting it on social media, and you can also encourage your audience to share your survey with their own networks. In general, people are more willing to complete surveys that are fairly short, so you'll want to make sure that you are not taking up too much of their time. A nice way to increase participation and thank people for completing your survey is to offer an incentive, such as a discount code or loyalty reward upon completion. Another incentive could be simply allowing people to see the results of the survey, depending on the nature of the questions, of course. People are curious, and love to answer polls that reveal something about themselves or their community, so sharing the results publicly could be a great way to increase engagement. Because they're conducted online, many surveys have an interesting real-time component. For example, you could ask an audience to test out a new app, asking them questions about the experience as they go along. You can also often see the results as they come in.

While you definitely don't need to be an expert to create a simple survey, it's worth remembering that a survey that is badly designed is not going to produce the results that you are looking for.

9.4 CROWDSOURCING

Crowdsourcing is defined as the act of outsourcing tasks which would have been traditionally performed by employees of an organization, to a large outside group of people, typically through social media channels. Crowdsourcing has many different functions, some of which you are probably already familiar with. Possibly the most well known example of crowdsourcing is the Wikipedia website. Wikipedia is among the world's largest online reference sites, and its articles are written entirely for free by anonymous contributors from all around the world. That is to say, Wikipedia's content comes from the crowd, the online community. Another great example of crowdsourcing is Kickstarter, which is a crowd-sourced funding platform commonly used to raise money for creative projects. Talent shows such as American Idol commonly use crowdsourcing when they ask their TV audience to rate or evaluate performers by texting or calling a hotline. And, on a more serious note, crowdsourcing was a crucial factor in the organization of protests during the recent revolution in Egypt. Crowdsourcing has also been highly effective in organizing disaster relief efforts.

Social Media is ripe for crowd sourcing. *Source:* www.dailycrowdsource.com[45]

Threadless is a T-shirt company that relies on customer votes to know which designs to print. People submit designs, and the ones with the most votes get printed.

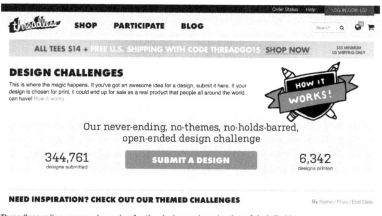

Threadless relies on crowdsourcing for the design and production of their T-shirts.
Source: www.threadless.com[46]

In terms of social media marketing, crowdsourcing has some very distinct advantages and benefits. First of all, you can get great solutions to problems from people who are already familiar with your product or industry. Secondly, you tap into an enormous reservoir of knowledge and talent that is out there in the world. Thirdly, you produce people who now have a vested interest in an outcome. When people have offered their input, they are typically eager to see (and possibly buy) the results.

Companies large and small have benefitted from crowdsourcing in a variety of ways. Pepsi's DEWmocracy campaign was a notable early success. Customers were asked to suggest and then vote on soft drink brand Mountain Dew's next flavor and packaging. The campaign was a huge success, with over one million people participating. Similarly, Vitamin Water used social media to crowdsource a new flavor and package design. Fans submitted their designs and voted via Facebook, Twitter, and blogs. The winner received $5,000, and when the new flavor (named "Connect") was launched, more than 100,000 people who had participated in the competition were eager to try it. Children's shoemaker Stride Rite held a competition for parents to create the ideal shoe for their children, even creating an app that the moms and dads could use in the design process.

Designs were submitted and thousands of people voted, and when the shoe was produced in 2011 the crowdsourcing community was eager to buy it. Sales numbers aside, all of these campaigns generated a huge amount of engagement and enthusiasm among fans, at little to no cost to the company.

Frito-Lay's "Do us a Flavor" campaign is another example: Using a Facebook app, the company invited users to create their very own flavor combos for a chance to win a cash prize of $1 million. Users around the United States submitted 3.8 million, almost four times the original goal of 1 million flavor submissions. Over 2.7 million users installed the Lays app on their phones, and the campaign added 2.2 million new Facebook fans for Frito-Lay's. More importantly, year-over-year sales increased by 12%, which was four times the goal for the campaign.

Frito Lay's "Do Us a Flavor" crowdsourcing campaign.
Source: www.dailycrowdsource.com[47]

Your company doesn't have to be as huge as Pepsi, Vitamin Water, Stride Rite, or Frito-Lay to benefit from crowdsourcing. You can easily crowdsource all kinds of suggestions and input, simply by asking a question like "What kind of shoes should we make?" You could also crowdsource the content that you share on social media platforms. For example, you could invite customers to pin photos of themselves wearing your company's clothes and then tag your brand, sharing the images in an online collection or Pinterest board. This is also a great way to get to know your audience. If you're an author with a reasonable following on Twitter, you could ask your followers to choose which title they like best for your next book.

CHAPTER 10

CREATING AND ADDING VALUE

10.1 SHARING EXPERTISE

Sharing expertise about your field, industry, or product can be one of the best ways to create valuable content on social media. It might seem counterintuitive at first; you may be thinking "If I tell people what I know about gardening/interior design/tax laws, then they'll be able to do it themselves, and they won't need to hire me." However, that could not be further from the truth. Sharing expertise will benefit you and your company in a variety of ways.

First off, did *you* become an expert by reading an online article? No, probably not. Depending on your field, you most likely spent years studying in school, practicing, training, interning, doing research, and/or working in your industry and gaining firsthand experience. Your clients and potential customers are not going to pick all that up overnight either, so don't worry that telling others what you know will make you replaceable. For example, if you own a landscaping business and you write a blog post with the title "How to Protect Your Garden from Winter Weather," you are sharing your expert knowledge with your community. Readers will certainly benefit from this information and look favorably on your business. But that doesn't mean they have the time, know-how, or tools to landscape their whole yard! When it's time for that project, they'll call you.

Secondly, high-quality content is the kind that people are most likely to share with their own social networks. Imagine that one of the people who follow your blog is an avid gardener, and reposts your "Winter Weather" article on his Facebook page, where 300 of his friends (many of whom also enjoy gardening) will see it. Maybe a couple of those friends repost it as well, or start to follow your blog and find other things they enjoy. That is a great way to increase word of mouth about your business. Not only that, but sharing expertise is a great way to increase your visibility in search results. For example, as the owner of the landscaping service, I write a series of articles about related topics, such as seasonal gardening tips, local wildflowers, endangered species, natural pesticides, tree pruning tips, and veggies at the local farmers' market. When someone searches for natural pesticides and they come across my article, they may become interested enough to look into my business, perhaps stopping by or even just remembering the name for later.

Thirdly, and perhaps most importantly, when you share your expertise, you have the opportunity to gain credibility in your community, create trust and loyalty with your customers, and position yourself as a leader in your industry. Sharing expertise gets your name out there, and improves your reputation, without coming across as an advertisement or a piece of marketing. Be authentically helpful, and let the world see your hard work, creativity, skills, and passion. Remember that social media is more about "attracting" customers than about "selling" a product! Remember that's its very similar to dating. Remember to LOVE: Listen, Offer, Visit, and Engage.

There are many ways to share your expertise, such as becoming a mentor or advisor, writing articles or opinion pieces, sharing resources, holding a workshop or conducting a training session, or volunteering to take the lead on a project or in a group, among others. And, of course, on social media there are just as many ways to share your experience and expertise; consider writing a blog post, sharing a video or interview, or podcasting.

10.2 SOLVING A PROBLEM

One of the main reasons that people go online is to search for the solution to some kind of problem or to figure out how to do something. If you can think about the kinds of problems that your customers might be having and then post a solution or suggestion, you have not only created useful, valuable content, but you have also brightened someone's day and helped them with a real-life issue.

The first step is to define your target audience and determine their potential problems. At this time, having well-thought-out buyer personas or brand heroes should be really helpful in understanding your actual or potential customers. (Remember that a buyer persona is a fictional profile that you create, based on data about your customers, to generate insight about their wants, needs, and habits.) For example, if my business is a veterinary clinic, a buyer persona might be "Urban Dog Owner" (of course, complete with relevant details about age, income, lifestyle, etc.). What problems might urban dog owners be experiencing? Can't find a pet-friendly apartment? Neighbors complaining about a barking dog? Got fleas? Need to hire a dog walker? Okay, I'll choose one of these and make a short YouTube video called "How to Get Your Dog to Stop Barking." When the urban dog owner finds my video in a Google search, he'll be happily relieved, and impressed by how friendly and knowledgeable the vet seems. Later on down the line, when his dog needs shots, he'll remember the vet from the video, look me up (he will of course have no trouble easily finding my contact information, because I have a Google+ business page), and make an appointment. Remember to provide clear information and links on whatever problem-solving content you share, so that interested clients can easily find your business or website.

If you think about this from the customer's point of view, it makes a lot of sense. Think about your own preferences as a customer. Would you be drawn to a website featuring someone pushing a product, and telling you how great they are? Probably not, and you probably would not spend much time looking at such a page. On the other hand, if you found a social media page or website that helped you solve a problem in some way—a site that was really useful to you—you'd probably explore more content on that page, or visit it again in the future.

Although this is not marketing per se, it's worth being aware of some other ways social media is used to solve real-world problems. Online activism and various relief efforts coordinated and shared via social media have achieved impressive results, both in the United States and abroad. For example, the Stop Online Piracy Act (SOPA) was recently scrapped after 3.9 million tweets against it were registered. In India, in less than 36 hours 500,000 people signed an online petition to clean-up government corruption, and a week later the government complied by agreeing to an anti-corruption law. The CIA as well as various law enforcement bureaus actively monitor a variety of social media to keep up-to-date with public sentiment. Governments, nonprofits, and activists are increasingly using social media because of the ease with which information can be shared from all sides. New uses for social media are being developed daily; maybe one of these new uses is relevant to your business, so keep an eye on the changing trends.

Last but not least, have you considered crowdsourcing? Remember that social media is a two-way street: You don't only need to solve your customers' problems; see if the public can also help you solve a problem for yourself! Ask for input and suggestions, or run a contest. This can be a great way to boost engagement.

10.3 TELLING STORIES

In the past, people bought and sold things face-to-face. You could evaluate who to trust by looking them in the eye, or by a firm handshake. You would know a vendor's reputation by word of mouth. You could examine the product for yourself, and if there was any problem you could go directly back to the source. And a marketplace or shop could be a fun place where neighbors met to chat, compare opinions, or share news. In many ways, social media replicates and mirrors the old marketplace experiences of the past, with the key word being *social*. Via social media, customers decide which companies are trustworthy, and they share word-of-mouth recommendations. They evaluate the quality of products and services online, and also give immediate feedback if there's a problem. And, like a traditional small-town marketplace, social media is a space where people gather to connect, interact, share information, and share stories.

Sharing stories is an essential way to both personalize your brand and also to get to know you customers and clients. A story can also be a vehicle to get and keep people's attention, and on social media there are so many ways to communicate—writing or blogging, a photo series, or a video, for example. Every company, no matter how dry or boring the industry might seem, has a story to tell. A good example was recently shared in class by one of my students, regarding Method Products. Their unique value proposition is that their products are nontoxic and clean. They have a story about a kid who drank a whole bottle of their liquid soap as a dare, and he then called the company to see if he was really going to be all right. He asked if they had any recommendations for him. They told him he would be fine, and recommended that he drink a lot of water. A cleaning product safe enough to drink is definitely something worthy of sharing.

Here are some potential topics for stories you can tell your audience: How did your company start? What is the history of your company? How did you survive changes in your industry or economic hardships? What interesting developments, inventions, or technological changes have occurred? What kinds of funny or interesting things happen on a typical workday? Who are your employees and what are their stories? Does your company participate in charitable events, volunteer work, or community organizations? Who are your customers?

This last one leads us to our next point: Invite your customers to share their stories as well. What is it that your company or product does that is unique, special, amazing? Who is passionate about your brand, and which social media platforms do they use? Who are your loyal customers and *why*? Give your customers plenty of opportunities to share their stories and experiences, for instance by creating a forum, group, fan page, or by simply posting a prompt or a question such as "How do you use our product?" You may also want to offer your audience incentives to share their stories. Some companies recognize their most loyal customers by sharing their stories widely in a feature such as "Fan of the week/month." Other companies offer competitions or prizes for the best story from a customer.

Many overworked business owners find that they no longer have much time to interact personally with the people around them; it's increasingly difficult (if not downright impossible) to connect with colleagues and customers on an individual level. Sharing stories on social media is a very human way to get to know your virtual neighbors. And there is an emotional component to it that increases engagement, interaction, and loyalty.

10.4 ANSWERING QUESTIONS

Asking and answering a question is one of the most fundamental aspects of interpersonal engagement, and this is no less true in the world of social media. Let's consider the following two sentences:

- Social media is fascinating.

- Do you think social media is fascinating?

In the first statement, I'm just telling you what to think. Your response is probably limited to "yeah," "um, sure," or "OK." But in the second sentence, the question has opened up a dialogue with you, and you can give me any number of responses. You can express your opinion, and you are much more actively engaged in a conversation. Furthermore, the first statement can come across as a bit presumptuous, but with the question I have demonstrated that I care about listening to you, not just in telling my side of the story, and this creates goodwill in our relationship.

Asking and answering questions on social media is a great way to get to know your audience and to let them know more about you as well. You can easily get feedback, do research, and test ideas, by posing interesting questions to your online community. Customers often prefer to respond when it's quick and easy; some popular question formats are yes/no questions, preference questions, opinion questions (e.g., "What's your favorite . . . ?"), knowledge or trivia challenges ("Can you guess where our new location is?"), or fill-in-the-blanks. For more in-depth responses, you could also invite customers to participate in a survey. You can try asking questions about your products and services, about customer perceptions, attitudes, and opinions, their knowledge of your products or brands, perceptions about your competitors, and so on. Research-and-development departments often spend a ton of money on marketing research, surveys, and focus groups, but if you have a healthy social media community, you can tap into public opinions and preferences for free.

Asking questions can also provide you with a great opportunity to address customer problems and concerns, as long as you actually listen to your online audience and respond or take appropriate actions in a timely fashion. Good questions include: "What products/services/flavors/colors, etc. would you like to see?" "What was your best/worst experience with our company?" "What can we do to improve our product/service?" "What do you think of our recent product/advertisement/announcement?"

Another helpful idea is to use a question-and-answer format to educate and inform your audience, or to answer commonly asked questions. For example, at the end of an announcement, advertisement, or blog post, you could provide a space for Q&A. Or, you could write a blog post that explains a typical problem or answers a frequently asked question, and then save time in the future by providing a link to that blog post whenever someone asks the same question.

Overall, asking questions is a way to keep your social media presence customer-centric. You can provide help and useful information, address concerns, and learn about your customers. You can guide a conversation without being forceful, and show that your company values openness, honesty, and feedback.

10.5 SPARKING DISCUSSIONS

With so much content out there on the Internet, how will you manage to grab your audience's attention? This is very much a problem we all face in real life, as well as in the realm of social media: What gets people talking? What is the best way to start a conversation that your audience will want to continue? You'll need to be creative, innovative, even provocative in order to pique your customers' interest and keep them coming back for more.

As detailed above, the first and easiest step to starting a great conversation is asking an intriguing question. You could easily begin an online discussion by asking your audience what they want, need, or like. Think of anything you might want to know from a market test or focus group, and try asking the online community in order to gain some insight about your customers. People are often more than happy to share their opinions, and they have a lot to say! Similarly, you could try crowdsourcing or asking for public input to solve a problem or make a decision.

Sharing breaking news is also a proven way to start discussions. This does not necessarily mean breaking world or national news; think about news in your company or industry. You can inform the public of new developments, products, changes in staffing or leadership, and events related to your field. Encourage the public to interact or offer an opinion by asking, "What do you think? Tell us in the comments." Or, if your company is a small business and your online followers are mostly local, you could certainly discuss events in your community or news that affects your clients in some way.

Sometimes, our most creative ideas come from brainstorming. Let loose, forget about the "right" and "wrong" answers, and just generate a list of topics you think your target audience might like to talk about— even things that have nothing to do with your brand directly. From there, you can write posts and questions that should generate discussions. Don't be afraid to experiment or go slightly off-topic!

A great example comes from the Omaha Steaks company. As you can imagine, after a while it became difficult to find exciting content about steaks. Eventually, they came up with the concept of "Table Talk"—that is, what do people talk about when they're having a meal together? They began to post an ongoing series of "Table Talk" questions about topics of general interest, designed to stimulate a lively conversation, and their online fans responded.

Remember that this is not only discussion for the sake of discussion. The number of likes or comments some content receives also helps determine how widely that content is seen; more likes and comments will drive that content to the top of people's newsfeeds, or a higher position in search results, thereby increasing visibility and awareness of your brand.

10.6 CREATING A SPECIAL OFFER

Everyone loves to save money, right? So, does it naturally follow that you should offer as many discounts as possible to your online followers? The answer, surprisingly, is maybe not always. Customers have been flooded for years with offers of "huge sales" and "valuable coupons" and "big savings inside," and many have grown savvy to the nature of marketing. A discount of 5–10% off is just not that impressive; most customers these days will not see that as a major value. Discounts of 50% or greater are generally seen as actually worthwhile, and are increasingly being used to attract new customers, or reward loyal fans. While it's true that many people who use social media will "like" or follow a page in order to get access to special offers, it's also true that there are millions of companies out there offering "valuable discounts," so offering coupons alone is not going to set you apart from the competition in any meaningful way. In other words, discounts are nice but they should not form the basis of your social media strategy.

First off, make sure your offer is optimized for relevancy, context, and target audience to avoid a "spammy" or junk-mail feel. People will actually "unlike" or unsubscribe from your feed if you constantly bombard them with useless, irrelevant, or low-value "deals." Consider carefully the timing of your offer, and what kinds of discounts or promotions will actually be of value to your audience.

Second, make sure that your offer is simple and user-friendly, and that the buying process is streamlined. Nothing is more annoying to customers than trying to redeem a special offer only to end up wasting time in the checkout process or ultimately discover that it doesn't work.

Third, make your offer of sufficient value that customers are willing to complete whatever task is asked of them in return. For example, would you complete a three-question survey for a 40%-off coupon to your favorite store? Probably, because it doesn't take too much of your time and the discount is good. Would you be willing to complete a 45-minute survey for a 5%-off coupon? No! Not worth it.

There are so many types of special offers and promotions; try thinking of the sales you typically see when you are shopping: Buy one, get one free (BOGO), a specific percentage off, free gift with purchase, discounted or free service, refer a friend and receive a discount, free parking, and so on. Another possibility is to offer a "deal of the week" or a regularly recurring contest.

Also, with the immediacy of social media, many companies are offering "flash" deals, in which followers can receive a deal if they respond quickly. For example, "First ten people to comment on this post get a free pizza!" or "Come in by 5:00 pm today and mention this ad for a free gift bag."

Last but not least, nobody argues with free. Remember that social media is all about sharing! Just like you were taught in preschool, sharing really is caring. Remember to Listen, Offer, Visit, and Engage.

10.7 SHARING A SPECIAL OFFER

When it comes to sharing the special offer or promotion that you have developed, there are a number of routes you could take. In recent years, we have seen the rise of social buying with companies like Groupon and LivingSocial, which offer special prices, packages, and coupons that go into effect only when a certain number of people commit to buying. The principle is that a company receives a lower profit margin for a particular item, but a larger sales volume, exposure to a lot of new clients, and, presumably, increased word of mouth. The social buying company (Groupon or Living Social) also takes a cut of the revenue from an already discounted item, so in some cases businesses are not left with much in the way of profit. However, many businesses feel that the potential buzz and new customers are worth the temporarily low profits.

One solution is to skip the social buying middleman, and offer the group sales directly to your customers via Facebook, Twitter, or another platform if they buy in sufficiently large numbers. There are apps (for example, Shopify) that you can use to manage such a sales strategy on Facebook.

Another popular approach is to offer special sales tied to social media action such as, for example, "If this post gets 500 likes, we'll offer 50% off" or "Share this page with 5 friends and receive 40% off your next purchase." Many of these special offers are designed to increase your visibility. You'll need to be realistic about the expectation, and then actually deliver the sale or promotion.

Keep in mind that Facebook has algorithms that determine which content is featured prominently in people's feed; the more likes and comments a post gets, the longer it remains at the top of the feed. In order to make sure people actually see your special offer and maximize your impact on Facebook, try combining buying opportunities with engaging content, like a question or an invitation to comment. For example, you could pose a fun question such as "Who do you think was the best-selling author in 2014?" combined with a promotion: "Post your guess in the comments section below! Then, click the link for 50% off books at our store."

10.8 SHARING HINTS, TIPS, AND TUTORIALS

Sharing hints, tips, and tutorials is one of the best ways to generate great content, and one of the best things you can do for your brand. In fact, marketers refer to content that will basically never go out of style (often educational or instructional material) as "evergreen" content. This is the kind of content that remains useful for a long time, or can be updated and refreshed in such a way that it stays relevant. Evergreen content is rich material that can be reposted or referenced again and again. It's usually good for generating both online and real-world conversations, and has strong pass-along value. In other words, your audience is quite likely to talk about it and share it, because it is useful. Well-made evergreen content can be a core element of your social media presence, and a backbone of your brand or image.

Consider, when possible, creating educational or tutorial material, hints or how-tos, and tips for beginners. You may want to create a series, page, or segment called "Getting Started" or "_____ for Beginners." People who are new to any activity are especially likely to be searching online for help; make sure that when they search, they find you and not your competitor. Increase the likelihood that people searching for a tutorial will find yours by choosing a clear and concise title, with an appropriate description and keywords.

By producing content that explains, teaches, or shows how something works, your brand can become a point of reference and a trusted online resource. As discussed previously, demonstrating your knowledge and expertise can help you earn the loyalty of your customers and position you as a leader in your field. This does not necessarily have to be concrete, step-by-step technical instructions either. Everyone wants to earn more money, feel less stressed, live a healthier lifestyle, and achieve their goals, so hints and tips about how you've done it can simply be sharing what you have discovered to have worked for you along the way, with recommendations and lessons learned. If your audience sees that you're willing to give this kind of useful information away, it's very likely they will indeed pay you for your expertise at another time, because they already know you have the experience.

Finally, consider your buyers' preferred media and learning styles. Some people would prefer to read a tutorial in written format, as in a blog post. Other people don't like to read, and would prefer to watch a video where they can see someone demonstrating how to do something. To the extent that it's possible, you should provide your material in several different formats. For example, if you create a YouTube video of a seminar, you could also provide a written transcript for those who learn better by reading. Even if the information is basically the same, different people will be attracted to different media.

For example, if you own a snowboarding shop you could film a five-minute video tutorial with one of your instructors, called "Snowboarding 101," that explains the most basic equipment and techniques. You could repost this video again at the beginning of the snowboarding season every winter, and also refer anyone who has a question to this video. If someone searches online for "how to snowboard," they'll find you. And you could provide written instructions with illustrations of the same material.

Another reason to post with both text and a video is that search engines will be more likely to rank your post higher if it has both video or voice and text, so not only can you reach both the people who prefer to read and the people who prefer to watch, but you can also attract people who don't yet know you exist.

10.9 SHOWING BEHIND THE SCENES

We all use social media to connect with other humans. We have a natural curiosity to know more about the lives and jobs of other people. Often, when it comes to business transactions, we choose to work with companies that we feel some sort of connection with. Sharing "behind the scenes" stories about your company and employees is a great way to humanize your business, intrigue your viewers, and establish a connection. There are probably more stories to tell about the fascinating people you work with and the amazing things that happen behind the scenes at your company, as well as more ways to tell those stories, than you may have imagined.

The first thing that comes to mind is perhaps sharing with your audience details of how a product is made. You could explore the research, testing, experimenting, or designing that goes into creating a new product. Or, you could show the physical process of how something is made or assembled. You could also show your facilities or offices. This even works for seemingly "boring" items, because the general public often has

Showcasing your employees is a great way to help people feel like you are more human.
Source: www.facebook.com[48]

no idea where everyday things that we take for granted actually come from, and are surprised to find out. This is ideal for anything designated as "craft" or "handmade," where your audience may be really concerned with the care and labor that goes into a product. Here is an opportunity to show off technology, workmanship, and quality.

Even if you don't produce a physical product, there are still so many "behind the scenes" stories to tell. A great place to start is by profiling your staff or employees. Who are they, and what do they do in your company? What is a typical day at work like? What is interesting about their job? Can they share some funny anecdotes? You could do a regular feature such as "Employee of the Week," or focus on specific departments. This may be especially helpful in industries where the real product is the knowledge, expertise, or service of an individual. Use a behind the scenes piece to highlight what makes this person so good at their job! You may remember from the discussion of images that, in general, people respond favorably to images of smiling faces making eye contact, so including photos or videos of your genuinely happy employees is great if it is an option.

Authenticity and transparency are two key concepts in social media marketing, and sharing behind the scenes media is a wonderful way to open your company to the online world. By sharing genuine, endearing content, you will increase engagement with your audience, who will be much more likely to choose you over a brand they have no connection with.

10.10 FUNNY IMAGES

Everybody likes to laugh, and while we don't all agree on what's funny or not, if you can get somebody to laugh, they will be much more likely to remember your advertisement or content. Humor is a fantastic way to popularize your brand without the aggressive marketing feel of more straightforward advertising. If you're in a highly competitive or saturated industry, humor can help you stand out from all your competitors. Similarly, if you're in a relatively "boring" industry, humor can really add some personality and charm to your content. Through humor you can even change the way that the public perceives your company.

For example, most people are familiar with GEICO car insurance's "gecko" and "caveman" commercials. Usually, car insurance is one of the least exciting and least humorous things in life; in fact, I would venture to guess that car insurance is mostly associated with all things tedious, complicated, and annoying. However, GEICO has had great success with their popular and funny commercials starring the anthropomorphic lizard and the talking caveman, which are hilarious, quirky characters, as well as with several other campaigns that used satire, parody, or other forms of humor.

Several other seemingly "boring" companies have also done well using humor. Charmin (toilet paper) was recently voted the "sassiest brand on Twitter" for their #tweetFromTheSeat campaign. Clorox (bleach) is a decades-old company that has reinvented itself with its "bleachable moments" campaign, which features real-life yet hilarious situations where bleach would come in handy.

Charmin is being (charmingly) funny with their #tweetFromTheSeat campaign on Twitter.
Source: www.twitter.com[49]

Another way to add humor to your brand is to have a celebrity comedian as a spokesperson, as in the Wonderful Pistachios Super Bowl 2014 ads featuring late-night host Stephen Colbert. It should go without saying that your funny ads, campaigns, or images can be used across a variety of social media.

A final note—it's best to avoid offensive humor. While it's okay to be a little gross (as in the Charmin and Clorox campaigns), a little bit shocking, provocative, silly, or weird, it's generally not a good idea to be derogatory, insulting, or otherwise insensitive. Always consider your target audience.

Cisco
February 14 · 🌐

Will you be our geek? Hope you're enjoying the day with someone you share a strong connection with. #ValentinesDay

Like · Comment · Share · 👍 187 💬 1 ↪ 27

Cisco knows their audience is people who consider themselves geeks and thrive in the computer connectivity industry. *Source:* www.facebook.com[50]

10.11 CONTESTING

The best way to achieve high levels of engagement is to offer your audience members an incentive to participate. Contests are an excellent way to do that, because most people love to play games, and who doesn't like to win something? Running contests on social media can take some planning, but it could also be something as easy as a Haiku contest like the one King Oscar Seafood offers on Facebook, or a simple vote with your hashtag entry. It's a good idea to offer a substantial prize and make entry relatively easy, or your contest will have very few entries. Facebook requires that contests are run through third-party applications right now, but they are relatively easy and inexpensive to set up. Woobox and Votigo, among many others, also offer contesting capabilities.

Backun Musical Services ran a 12 Days of Backun contest, with a grand prize of an all-expenses-paid trip to ClarinetFest 2015 in Madrid, Spain. In order to be entered for a chance to win, each person had to "like" the

The Backun Musical Services page offered a substantial contest prize: An all-expenses-paid trip for two to Madrid for ClarinetFest. *Source:* www.facebook.com[51]

original post and comment, as well as "like" and comment on each of the 12 Days of Backun. This, in turn, grew Backun Musical Services' likes significantly during the contest, because all of the clarinet fans of Backun were liking and commenting in order to try to win the prize. Not only was the contest well-aligned with the Backun Musical Services audience of clarinetists, but it was also a fun way to get to know the brand and the various artists who play on Backun clarinets. Backun also asked questions of participants in order to find out more about them. They were definitely listening, offering, visiting, and engaging with their community for the contest, and they continue to do so on all their social channels. You don't have to be a big brand to offer something amazing to your potential customers.

Backun Musical Services also encouraged engagement while getting to know their audience by asking them several questions. *Source:* www.facebook.com[52]

CHAPTER 11

ADVANCED HACKS

11.1 USING POPULAR MEMES

The word "meme" was originally coined by ethologist and evolutionary biologist Richard Dawkins, and in the simplest terms it refers to "an idea, behavior, or style that spreads from person to person within a culture." In the same way that genes transmit genetic information, a meme can be considered a way of transmitting cultural information. In the world of the Internet and social media, "meme" is commonly used to refer to a popular image, phrase, joke, or trend that is constantly evolving through repetition, adaptation, and sharing. Often, a meme contains a well-known character, with a caption that sharers adapt to their needs. You have most likely seen a meme, even if you didn't know that's what it was, as they are often the type of content that is posted on Facebook, Instagram, and other social media. Popular recent memes include Grumpy Cat, Dancing Baby, First World Problems, Nuts the Squirrel, LOL Cats, Throw Back Thursday (#TBT), #YOLO (You Only Live Once), the Ice Bucket Challenge, and the Dos Equis beer guy, and right now we may be going through a *Fifty Shades of Gray* meme.

Memes are not generally considered "high quality" content, and, as such, they shouldn't form the core of your social media content. However, they are pretty harmless and popular, so occasional use of memes should be fine. And, in fact, it's important to understand how memes work if you want to stay current with emerging trends. Some marketers have successfully used memes as a low-cost way to create a

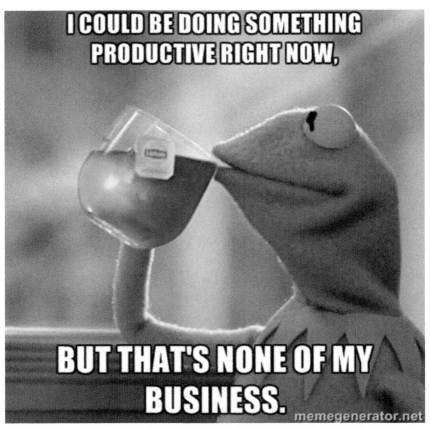

I COULD BE DOING SOMETHING PRODUCTIVE RIGHT NOW,

BUT THAT'S NONE OF MY BUSINESS.

memegenerator.net

An example of a meme image generated by memegenerator.com. *Source:* www.memegenerator.net[53]

buzz, or demonstrate awareness of quickly-shifting online fads. Memes can be a handy way to stay relevant or quickly generate content that fans will respond to.

One of the main benefits of memes is that they are cheap and easy to create (there is even a website called memegenerator.net). They are also quick and easy to view, often consisting of just a picture and a few words. Remember that highly visual content is ideal for social media. They feature familiar and highly-identifiable themes or characters. They establish an emotional connection with the viewer by using humor, and often make people feel that they are "in" a specific community or culture that shares a common reference point. They are easy and fun to share; if a meme makes people laugh they are quite likely to "like," share, or repost it, so make sure your meme is optimized with the appropriate buttons to facilitate sharing. And, they are based on a joke or image that is already hugely popular. Rather than trying to create something from scratch, you can leverage the fact that a meme is already a viral trend.

The tricky part of using memes is that you have to be sure that you get the joke first. You have to understand the way the meme is used, what it communicates, and what kinds of punch lines are appropriate. You also need to consider your audience; if they are not familiar with a particular meme, the joke could fall flat. Memes tend to work best with young, Internet-savvy audiences. Timing is essential when using a meme. You need to catch it while it's still rising in popularity, but before it gets boring or is used by some other company. You also want to make sure that it's a meme that is in some way relatable to your company—don't choose a meme that makes no sense just because you think it's hilarious. As with other forms of humor, you need to be careful that you're not choosing a potentially offensive meme.

Last but not least, memes (like most social media content) are not entirely under your control, so there's the potential for them to go off in an unwanted direction. Keep this in mind if there's some controversy about your company that could turn ugly. A good example of this was provided by the recent Bill Cosby meme generator. It featured a cheerful picture, and invited the public to create their own memes. His PR team were certainly hoping for some friendly and wholesome content, but, instead of that, the public used the meme to express outrage and disgust at the actor over serious allegations of rape. The meme generator was quickly deleted, but the point had been made.

11.2 NEWSJACKING

Newsjacking is the strategy of inserting your company or concepts into a breaking news story. You are essentially leveraging current events for the promotion of yourself or your brand. The basic idea is that, as a news story is breaking, journalists will be searching for relevant information, which is where you come in by producing some content that will lead reporters to you. Then, with any luck, your brand will be mentioned in media coverage related to the news item. There are many ways to do this, which we will discuss in more detail below. A key point is that newsjacking depends to a great degree on immediacy—you need to be following current events and responding in real time. Lets look at some examples of how it works.

One of the most talked-about incidents of newsjacking occurred during the 2013 Super Bowl, when a blackout halted the game for 35 minutes. Oreo (yes—the cookies brand) responded almost immediately by posting a simple picture of an Oreo cookie against a nearly black background with the caption "You can still dunk in the dark." Although Oreo has no direct connection to football, people were impressed by their fast and witty response. That post received nearly 20,000 likes, 790 comments, and over 6,500 shares. Furthermore, the media picked up on the story and discussed Oreo's clever strategy during their coverage of the blackout, thereby generating even more publicity and conversation. Oreo has since become a brand to mimic in social media, and they continue to live up to their great reputation.

Oreo's "You can still dunk in the dark" tweet during the 2013 Super Bowl has become the ultimate example of real-time marketing. *Source:* www.wired.com[54]

Newsjacking is not only used by businesses; for instance, the PR team of Barack Obama has pulled off some notable instances of newsjacking as well. In 2012 President Obama joined Instagram (@BarackObama) on the exact same day as the Republicans' Iowa Caucus. Political journalists were out in force for the caucus, but Obama's Instagram account became the big news of the day, effectively diverting a bit of attention from the Republican candidates.

The first step to effective newsjacking is to keep an eye on the news. You may want to start by following important people or feeds, monitoring keywords, or setting up alerts (such as Google Alerts) so that you know when your business or something related comes up in the news or in social media platforms. You may also want to keep an eye on what's trending on Twitter and/or look at PopURLs.com or Google Trends. Then, when a relevant story starts to develop, you'll need to be ready to seize the moment. One easy way to let people know you have something to say is to comment or reply to others' posts, perhaps including a link or your contact information. Similarly, you can monitor stories on Twitter, and then post relevant tweets using the appropriate hashtags to join in the conversation.

Journalists will be searching for sources of information to fill in the details, gather background information, or add perspective to a story. You can position yourself to be found and interviewed by the media by immediately writing a relevant blog post, tweet, or shooting a video of, for example, a speech or press conference. Because search engines (Google, Bing, etc.) now index in real time, whatever content you have posted will appear in search results right away and hence will be available to journalists. To maximize your chances of getting noticed in a search, use appropriate keywords and titles. If they are interested in what you have to say, or if you can provide some information relevant to their story, they may contact you or at least mention your post, video, etc. This strategy works by putting your voice or opinion out in the world, and then waiting to see if the media becomes interested in the course of their investigations. However, you can also send your message directly to the media by using tip lines or features such as CNN's iReport. Or you can tweet comments directly to reporters, or engage in citizen journalism in your own neighborhood. The OnPublico app is working to facilitate this.

One word of caution: not all news stories are marketing opportunities. While you do not always need a direct link to current events to say something interesting or relevant (see the Oreo example), you do need to keep it in good taste, and use good judgment. For example, during Hurricane Sandy, *InStyle* magazine offered a cosmetics package with the title "Hurricane Sandy Have You Stuck Inside? 5 Beauty Treatments to Help Ride Out the Storm." This was widely perceived as crass, trivial marketing on the back of a natural disaster that tragically killed more than 200 people. It was a bad idea, disrespectful, and damaging to the brand. On the other hand, Duracell set up mobile phone charging centers to help people who lost power during the storm, and used their Facebook page to provide updates about their location. The media and the public took notice, and Duracell received a lot of positive coverage.

11.3 MICRO-TARGETING AUDIENCES

There is a current theory, known as the "long tail" of marketing, which posits that our culture and economy (due in a large part to the advent of online retail) is moving away from producing mass-marketed, mainstream "hits," and is instead moving toward producing narrowly targeted goods and services that appeal to specialized, niche consumers. Amazon, iTunes, and Netflix are three enormous companies that have found success in providing not only mainstream hits, but also in catering to underserved niche markets as well, offering unique items that would not usually be found in a traditional physical store.

Micro-targeting can be defined as using demographics and consumer data to understand the needs of individuals or very small groups of like-minded people, and then to effectively market your product to them. Micro-targeting allows you to produce highly personalized messages that cater to very segmented audiences. One of the most important goals of micro-targeting is to identify the preferred communication channels and social media platforms of the target audience so that you can reach them more effectively. In the past, companies had to spend thousands of dollars to produce one-size-fits-all TV or print advertisements with mass appeal, which really spoke to nobody in particular. But with social media and online marketing, businesses have the power to skip traditional media and communicate directly with their audience via whatever network is just right for that particular audience.

In general, a great many customers will be using the major social media sites such as Facebook, Twitter, and YouTube, but, depending on your industry, you may find that some of your most passionate customers are also actively using smaller niche social networks. There literally is an online community for every conceivable interest, hobby, and lifestyle, so you should do some research into your target audience and meet them on their own turf.

For example, photographers might be really active on Flickr, gardeners are posting and chatting on YardShare.com, interior designers are active on Houzz, and dog lovers can be found on Dogster.com. These smaller networks are not always set up for businesses and advertising in the way that, say, Facebook is, but it is worth getting to know how they work. You will be casting a very small net, but the audience you attract can be really valuable, core customers. Your goal is to find your audience—wherever they may be—and then listen (offer, visit) and engage with them.

Besides social networks, review-style social sites, such as Angie's List, Yelp, or TripAdvisor may also be relevant, depending on your industry. You may not have much chance for marketing, but you should probably be aware of any reviews that are posted about your business on a niche review site, and respond to them as necessary. RSS (Really Simple Syndication) feeds and other news aggregators are also useful in micro-targeting and niche marketing, because they allow users to receive updates based on their needs and interests. Notably, Netflix offers RSS feeds, so that fans can receive news based on their specific tastes in movies. Rather than get spammed about every new blockbuster, I can choose to receive alerts based on my personal, specific interests—archaeological documentaries and Swedish language programs, for example.

Micro-targeting can be ideal for organizations such as churches, nonprofits, local businesses, musicians or artists' collectives, freelancers, or companies with unusual or specialized products, because you have the opportunity to provide targeted information directly to your niche audience at a fraction of the cost of traditional advertising. It has also become especially useful to political campaigns as a way to reach voters. Campaign managers have begun to collect and maintain databases of detailed information about individual voters, and, using demographics and predictive analytics, they can then create models of voter opinions. In this way they can speak to voters about specific issues that they are likely to be concerned with, rather than sending out blanket party statements. This personalized technique was notably used in the 2012 Presidential campaign. The more personalized your content and targeting can be, the better.

11.4 REPURPOSING MATERIAL ACROSS PLATFORMS

Social media has brought about truly significant changes in the way we produce and receive information. A piece of news that in the past might have been distributed as one unit, in one specific way, can now be posted as four or five separate bits of content. For example, 25 years ago, a company might have written a single press release to announce the launch of a new product. Today you could write a detailed blog post about your new product, or even several posts if you wanted to provide the story of its development, list its technical features, interview the designer, and explain how to use it. Then you could tweet brief announcements about the launch party the day before, and the day of.

Post photos of the new product on Instagram, along with a link back to your blog or webpage. Make a behind-the-scenes video before the product's launch, and afterwards make a video demonstrating how to use it. Post that video on YouTube and on your company's Facebook page. Make a cool infographic with some details about the item or your company, or even about similar products, and post it on Pinterest. Update your company's LinkedIn profile or add a Spotlight page to provide more information to your professional network, or even post on LinkedIn from your personal profile, since LinkedIn now offers longer posting capabilities.

While this might seem like overkill, remember that all of your customers or potential customers will not be following you on every form of social media. Even if they were, people generally only see a fraction of all the content that is posted, because of the way their newsfeeds are structured. For example, someone might follow your company on Facebook, Twitter, and Instagram, but they haven't logged in to Instagram since last July, and they have 750 friends on Facebook so your post got lost in the noise. That means that they only actually saw your tweet!

Furthermore, you will not be posting exactly the same content on each page—Instagram has a photo, while your blog has an article. The content will be adjusted, customized to reflect the culture of different social media sites. Producing different content is not only a cheap way to extend your marketing; it's an essential tool for reaching your audience. Remember that people have different learning styles, as well as different levels of interest in and understanding of your product. While some people would prefer to read, others like videos. For someone who is only tangentially interested in your product, a tweet might be all they need or want to know; an industry insider, on the other hand, will be eager to read all of the in-depth details. You can actually help the public and the media understand your product better by providing materials and information in a variety of formats to meet their needs.

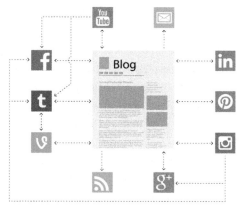

For repurposing content: your blog is the center, or hub and all other networks can be used to share content from the blog and also point back to the blog. *Source:* Suse Barnes

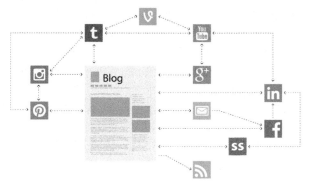

Your social media ecosystem. *Source:* Suse Barnes

Another way to create fresh content is to "spin" popular or detailed topics into multiple posts. Take one key concept or piece of information and write about it from a variety of different perspectives, or as a series. For example, I could take one topic, vegetarian cooking, and write "Vegetarian Cooking for Beginners," "Top 5 Tips for Vegetarian Meals," "Video: How to Make Vegetarian Lasagna," "The Vegetarian Revolution," and so on. This level of detail can be attractive to people who are hunting for quite specific advice.

If you are short on time and resources, you will definitely need to make the most of the content you have created. Here are just a few of many repurposing shortcuts that anyone can use. Start by choosing a solid piece of content, perhaps your "evergreen" content, or just some content that got a lot of likes or includes really great information. Then, create an outline or list of the main points, and share it on social media. Or, find a great one-line quote from the text or an interview, and use that to create a word-image to post on Instagram. Alternatively, you could tweet a great quote from the article, with a link back to the original post. Combine some statistics or data from a blog post with an image and post it on Facebook, or create an infographic to post on Pinterest.

11.5 TAGGING

Essentially, tags and hashtags are descriptive keywords that help people find your content in an online search, and they have a variety of functions. Tags can be created for different types of media; for example, audio files, videos, written posts, and photos can all be tagged. Tags can also help group material together or quickly tell your audience what a post or article is about. And tags can be used to identify individual people (or business entities) within a post or photo. Because tags are one of the main ways for people to find you, you'll want to make sure that you are tagging your content, and tagging it correctly.

Tags should be accurate, concise, and should thoroughly describe the content. For example, if I own a bookstore and I write a blog post about the best science-fiction novels for teens, I would probably add the tags "books," "science fiction," "teens," and "best of." That way, if someone searches for "science fiction for teens" or "best sci-fi," they are pretty likely to find my blog post. Tools like Google's Keyword Planner and UberSuggest.org will help you find which words are getting the most searches. As described in http://www.digitaltrainingacademy.com /casestudies/2012/12/converses_domaination_campaign_makes _innovative_use_of_paid_search_keyphrase_bidding.php, Converse actually ran several successful campaigns using the technique of finding what people are interested in at specific times of the year, and then building low-cost Google AdWords (paid search) campaigns connected to social media marketing in order to attract visitors to microsites. They called this strategy (or group of campaigns) Converse Domaination, and effectively led lots of their audience members to their various online properties. See http://youtu.be/CHtyQJzTy70.

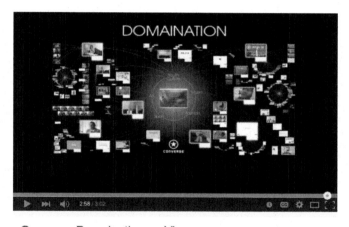

Converse Domaination on Vimeo

think with Google

think with Google

Subscribe 2,386

18,163

Watch the Converse Domaination video on YouTube at http://youtu.be/CHtyQJzTy70.
Source: www.youtube.com[55]

You need to think about what keywords your customers are likely to be searching for as well. For example, if I own a bike shop and I post a photo of the great new bikes we got in, I should tag it with useful key-words. While I identify the bike by its product number TX-490L, and I could include that in the tag, it's not likely that my customers will search for a "TX-490L." So, I should probably include layman's terms such as "mountain bike" or "10-speed bike" as well.

For longer posts, as well as videos, it may be helpful to come up with tags that describe each section or chapter. Many individuals and businesses also use a standard set of tags that they apply to all of the content they upload. For example, the bookstore owner might tag all of his content with "books" or "reading," and the bike shop owner might consistently use "cycling," "bikes," and "outdoor." It's also possible to add tags for social media sites such as Reddit, Digg, StumbleUpon, and Delicious, so that your release will be found there as well.

One of the confusing aspects of tags is that the same words may be used in different ways by different people. For example, the tag "bikes" could equally refer to kids' toys, ten-speeds, or Harley-Davidsons. New tags can also be added to old content. Hashtags (#) of the type used on Twitter and other platforms are included in this discussion of tags, as they can also be used to identify content and create categories.

On the more social end of the spectrum, tags can be used to identify people in photos or posts, and the person who has been tagged receives a notification. On a social media site, a person's friends would typically be able to see photos or posts that they are tagged in. People usually have the option to remove a tag if they don't want to be identified in a post.

PART

3

CHAPTER 12

THE 21 PRINCIPLES OF SOCIAL MEDIA

12.1 UNDERSTAND YOUR AUDIENCE

Perhaps more so than in any other part of your business (whether it's customer service, public relations, marketing, or sales), in social media it's imperative that you understand your audience. This translates to listening carefully to how they converse on their social networks, listening for what they find interesting, listening for trends, and listening for pain points. If you have listened to your audience well and you have reached a good understanding of who they are and what they want, you will then be ready to offer them the content and promotions that they will best respond to. Such a level of understanding will assist you with all aspects of your social media communications and campaigns, and it will be the foundation on which you make strategic decisions about how to engage with your audience. Think of your customers as your friends, and converse with them in a friendly and respectful manner. Remember that people trust their friends much more than they trust an impersonal business; as a result, people would much rather do business with people they know and trust than partner with an unknown entity. Understanding your audience will allow you to show that you care, nurture your relationships with customers and potential customers, and learn what they are looking for. Your audience will ultimately define your brand and your product offerings, because they are the ones who are willing to pay for them; therefore it behooves you to make them feel like you really "get" them.

Pinterest is a social network that is doing this very well. Talk to any Pinterest user, and they will tell you that Pinterest seems to understand what they like. Pinterest sends out emails with suggested pins and boards for their users to follow on a regular basis, and the Pinners are usually delighted with these suggestions. Pinners say, "They really get me," i.e. they usually feel that Pinterest's suggestions are excellent. This keeps Pinners engaged and happy, not to mention that it allows Pinterest to continue growing as a business. It's a symbiotic relationship.

Pinterest   Get the app!
                     Android · iOS

Hi Susby Internet Solutions,
We've found a few more things you might want to add to your new Color: Sea board:

More pins for your board

An email from Pinterest with more image suggestions for pinning to a recently created board.
Source: The author's email

12.2 BE AUTHENTIC

Many large companies these days suffer from the public's perception that they are impersonal, misleading, fake, uncaring, scripted, and dishonest; in a word, *inauthentic*. People want exactly the opposite of that in their personal lives as well as in their dealings with businesses in the real world and online. Authenticity is attractive to people, breeding trust and strengthening ties; but how can you make a brand or a company authentic?

First off, you need to identify your company's core values and desired image. When you are posting on social media or interacting with the public, you should remain more or less consistent with the personality of your company. That does *not* mean giving canned responses or following a cookie-cutter program, but simply communicating in a way that is genuine and true to your company's overall persona.

Social media is all about social interaction with real individuals. People do not want to be treated impersonally, like just so many cogs in a wheel. To the best of your ability, you should empathize with your customers and always try to relate to them as actual human beings. And, on the other side of the coin, let the public know that you are not some impersonal monolithic corporation, but a business made up of real people with real lives and interests. In this sense, behind-the-scenes content can be especially effective at humanizing your brand.

12.3 BE HONEST

As a customer, would you want to spend your money on a company that has lied to you, manipulated you, or sold you falsely advertised goods? Of course you wouldn't, so as a marketer you should not consider such tactics either. While companies obviously cannot tell everyone exactly what they are doing all the time, there are some pretty clear guidelines for honesty in the realm of social media.

The first rule is honesty of relationships. You must be clear about who you are working with or representing. The second rule is honesty of opinion, meaning that you should not be lying or exaggerating just in order to sell something. The third rule is honesty of identity. Don't pretend to be someone else; for example, on a blog or page where many people can post, authors should sign off with their initials or personal handle, so that it's clear who has written each piece.

If you have made a mistake, or encountered some kind of controversy, immediate and full disclosure is usually the best way of dealing with it. Not only is lying bad PR and unethical, it is also illegal in many situations, and you could potentially be fined by the FCC. However, the damage to your reputation would probably be much worse than any monetary fine. A good rule of thumb is that if you have to think about whether something is unethical or not, it probably is. So don't do it.

12.4 BE TRANSPARENT

In the age of the Internet, it is nearly impossible to hide the truth. Every single customer essentially has access to the world's store of information at their fingertips. Consumers expect more transparency from government, companies, and organizations than ever before. If you're considering launching a social media presence for your company, you need to be ready to face the facts about your products and your business model, as the public can and will discover all your dirty laundry.

Some general guidelines are as follows: If you are doing something that you don't want the public to know about, the solution is not to try to hide it, but rather stop doing it. Fix the problem at its source. If you are receiving money or promotional products from a company or client, be upfront about your relationship. Similarly, if you are offering customers products in exchange for positive reviews or endorsements, you must disclose that relationship as well. And, as mentioned above, you need to be clear about who is speaking, tweeting, or posting on behalf of your company.

Under no circumstances should you try to create a fake profile, or attempt to sneak corporate-sponsored material onto social media by misrepresenting it as something that was consumer generated. Practice full disclosure at all times.

12.5 BE CONSISTENT

In order to have a successful social media presence you will need to be consistent in your efforts over the long term. Many marketers make the mistake of posting some great content, but then giving up when there isn't an immediate response, or, even worse, when there is not a measurable ROI (Return on Investment). But this is not the way social media works; just like in real life, trust and relationships are only built up after repeated contact and consistently positive experiences. In order for social media marketing to succeed, you need to make a long-term commitment to delivering quality content on a regular basis. Here's where it's helpful to follow an editorial or content calendar. (See 12.19 for more on that.)

Also, your company should be consistent in its brand, personality, tone, and image. That is not to say that everything should be uniform—far from it. Uniqueness and spontaneity are, of course, key factors in social media. But your company should have a consistent, unified approach even if different people or teams manage different aspects of your marketing across different social media platforms. Your company's identity and core values should be clearly defined, and this should show in the language you use and the types of content you post. You may also want to create a consistent "signature" look by using specific colors, fonts, logos, or filters in your images.

12.6 BE ENGAGING AND INSPIRING

People don't want to be told what to think or be manipulated by marketing. The best way to win over potential customers and fans is to be engaging and inspiring; to routinely post content that attracts their attention or encourages their participation. Michael Stelzner's Social Media Examiner blog is a good example, and a very useful site for future reference as well; see www.SocialMediaExaminer.com.

The first step toward engagement is being a good listener—paying attention and asking lots of questions to learn more about your audience/community. You can help your audience get to know you by sharing stories about your company and the people that work there, or providing special behind-the-scenes peeks. People often turn to the Internet for helpful information, so sharing your expertise on a given topic, providing hints, tips, or tutorials, or helping people solve a problem are examples of the type of content that is very welcome. People become authentically engaged because they are interested in learning from you. Similarly, you could engage people by starting discussions about topics of interest. You can also boost engagement by creating opportunities for your fans to speak up, give feedback, get involved, or participate in a special event. What could be more engaging than building a community?

Inspiration, while hard to quantify, is something that many people are seeking on social media. We love to hear great stories about real people and their achievements. Be inspiring by sharing what makes your company amazing. What makes you passionate about your job? What exciting things are you doing that no other company does? What makes you unique? Sharing what you've learned is a wonderful way to inspire those around you.

12.7 BE APPROACHABLE AND EMOTIVE

People use social media in hopes of finding some sort of human connection, so your business should not present itself as a sterile, faceless corporate presence online. There are a lot of things you can do to humanize your business and make it more approachable.

First of all, don't be afraid to show the people who work behind the scenes to your fans. Profiling your employees and what they do is a great way for the public to get to know you. And, on the other hand, you can share your customers' true stories with the community. People respond strongly to images of humans smiling and making eye contact, so include such photos or videos if possible.

You may want to use other images too; keep in mind that the image does not necessarily have to be a picture of your product. What's more important is that the image conveys an emotion that you want your audience to experience and share, or to associate with your brand.

Try to speak, write, or post as naturally as possible, using a friendly and positive tone. You may even want to use emoticons to help convey feelings simply. :) But, above all, strive to be transparent, open, and authentic in all of your communications. If you demonstrate your true values and personality, your audience will likely want to engage with your content.

12.8 RESPOND QUICKLY TO NEGATIVE COMMENTS

You should always respond to negative comments as quickly as possible. Not responding sends the message that you simply don't care about your customers and their concerns. By not addressing negative comments you lose the opportunity to nip a problem in the bud, and you may be enabling a complaint to grow and spread out of control. Some top companies have a policy of responding in one hour or less; if this is not an attainable goal, even responding within 24 hours is better than nothing, and there are many apps and programs that can help you keep track of mentions of your company and alert you to incoming complaints. In any case, you need to dedicate serious time and effort to dealing with any negative comments that may be posted about your company.

Often, a simple apology or offer to communicate further in private can defuse the situation, as most customers just want to be heard and treated like a human being. If you cannot resolve the issue immediately, at least let the customer know that you have received their complaint and are working on it, and that you will get back to them with an answer as soon as possible.

Justin Searls
@searls   ⚙ Follow

Almost missed my connectio—I mean my
direct flight that magically stops in Chicago,
changes planes, gates, and concourses.
Thanks @united

RETWEETS   FAVORITES
7   16

2:41 PM - 5 Mar 2015

Reply to @searls @united

Sam Phippen @samphippen · Mar 5
@searls @united I'm in Chicago rn

Justin Searls @searls · Mar 5
@samphippen neat

Sam Phippen @samphippen · Mar 5
@searls #missedconnections

United @united · Mar 5
@searls A direct flight means that there is a stop & a possible change of
gates/planes. A non-stop flight means that there is no stop. ^GJ
            168   51

Johnny Winn @johnny_rugger · Mar 5
.@united @searls you keep using those words, I do not think they mean what you
think they mean
            11   44

Jared Fraser @modsognir · Mar 5
@united @searls what's an indirect flight then?
                      5

Evan Phoenix @evanphx · Mar 5
@united @searls What's the difference between a direct flight and a flight that
requires a transfer (indirect) then?
                      3

Scott Scoble @lvcodesmith · Mar 5
@united @searls that's idiotic
                      2

mark mceahern @m5rk · Mar 5
@united @searls I think you guys meant to have this conversation on April 1st,
right?
                      2

Justin Searls @searls · Mar 5
@united which English definition of the word "direct" describes the first
scenario? Sounds more like "disjoint", "connecting", or "indirect"
                      4

Caleb Thompson @calebthompson · Mar 5
@united @searls Please find a dictionary and get back to us re: "direct".

A tweet exchange between an unhappy customer on United Airlines and the
United twitter representative ^GJ, makes United look like they don't really
know what they are doing. *Source:* www.twitter.com[56]

12.9 RESPOND TO POSITIVE COMMENTS TOO

Many of us were taught as we were growing up that the gracious way to accept a compliment was simply to say "thank you." The same rule of basic etiquette applies to positive comments you will receive via social media. The first step is to thank the reviewer for their business and for taking the time to leave their feedback. If you have a lot of followers, or are fortunate enough to have many positive comments, you may only have time to respond with a quick "like" or "Thanks!"

However, if you have time for a longer response, it really helps show that you care about your customers. The wording and tone that you choose should match your identity as a company or brand. Compare the very casual "Thanks, dude! You rule." to the more formal "We value you as a customer and appreciate your feedback, sir."

A happier conversation helps build customer confidence and instill a feeling of goodwill in customers. *Source:* www.twitter.com[57]

You may want to reinforce a positive point that they've made, and encourage them to visit your business again, or, if it's relevant, let them know about another product they might enjoy. "Thanks, Tim. We're glad to hear you liked X. Have you tried Y?" Or, you could encourage them to help spread positive word of mouth: "Thanks. Please tell your friends about our page!"

Particularly positive comments can be shared externally (reposted on your page so that other viewers can see them) and internally, to boost morale or show your team that their hard work is appreciated.

12.10 NEVER DELETE A COMMENT

From time to time you will probably receive some negative comments on your social media pages, which you should respond to as quickly as possible. No matter how unfavorable the comment is, you should never, ever delete a legitimate complaint or criticism. This tends to make the complaining customer even angrier, and casts you in a bad light with your other fans as well. Keep in mind that in the age of social media, hitting "delete" does *not* make something disappear. Too many people will have already seen it and potentially taken a screenshot or in some other way saved the negative content. The only way to improve the situation is to address the problem honestly and responsibly.

There is one important exception to the "do not delete" rule, and that is content that is truly offensive—for example: racist, sexually explicit, profanity-laden, threatening, malicious, or violent comments. On your own social media pages, you can and should establish guidelines about what content is allowed, and then monitor carefully, removing offensive comments if necessary. This keeps the online community a welcoming place for everyone, and a place where legitimate complaints are acceptable. In extreme cases, it may even be necessary to document the offensive comment, delete it from the page, and block or report the commenter to the proper authorities.

...rk The internet has already recorded that you have no qualms posting the exact same customer information when it is good feedback and not a snide comment by a horrible person. When a lawyer gets wind of this, i would get ready to grab my ankles.

about a minute ago · via mobile · Like · 👍 1

...lo Really Applebee's? " Applebee's have strict policies to protect personal information -- even guest's names." If that were true then why did you post this!? Hypocrites! http://sphotos-b.xx.fbcdn.net/hphotos-prn1/19100_136476209851670_2070951401_n.jpg

34 minutes ago · Like · 👍 2

... What happens on the internet, stays on the internet. This was deleted not to long ago by applebees shortly after this issue went viral.

http://sphotos-b.xx.fbcdn.net/hphotos-prn1/19100_136476209851670_2070951401_n.jpg

2 hours ago · Like

Applebees deleted comments on Facebook and fans pointed it out to others interested in the story. *Source:* www.rlstollar.wordpress.com[58]

Applebee's had to contend with an onslaught of negative comments in early 2013 when an employee posted a photo of a bill from a pastor who had written on it "I only give God 10%, why should I give you 18%?" According to the R. L. Stollar (Overturning Tables blog's photo essay account of the incident, https://rlstollar.wordpress.com/2013/02/02/applebees-overnight-social-media-meltdown-a-photo-essay/), the story received over 1.4 million views on social media, demonstrating Applebee's lack of understanding of how best to handle a problematic situation that goes viral on social media.

12.11 QUICK PUBLIC RESPONSE, THEN TAKE IT PRIVATELY

In the world of social media, it is critical to monitor and respond to everything as much as possible. That includes the responses that the public will make to things that you post, as well as comments that they will make either on your site or on other sites in a discussion about you. While some companies hesitate to get involved in social media for fear of the negative comments and responses they might get, this is not actually a situation to fear as long as you have a solid plan for how to handle complaints. In fact, handling adversity well should serve to boost trust in your competence as an organization and increase goodwill.

If you're really concerned about negative comments, there are a few things you can do to prevent them before they happen. Make it as easy as possible for people to solve problems for themselves online, or to contact you directly to solve a problem. You can do this by creating a FAQ section, as well as easy access to email, private message, or appropriate phone numbers. Also, if there's some not-so-positive news about your company, you can use your social media profile as a way to break the news yourself, publish a response, and show that you are taking accountability and action. For a fairly complicated situation that may take some time to resolve, you should always respond publicly to the complaint, and then offer to discuss the matter in more detail privately. A message such as "I'm sorry to hear you've had a bad experience. Please contact my office at xxx-xxxx and I will be happy to assist you" should suffice.

Most of these kinds of comments happen in the airline industry, but here's an example from CVS.

A non-airline example of a customer complaint and company response on Twitter.
Source: www.twitter.com[59]

12.12 HOW TO PRIORITIZE CUSTOMER RESPONSE

Depending on the size of your company and the number of followers you have, it may be realistically impossible to address all customer complaints instantly. This is especially true if you are in a troubled industry with a lot of unhappy customers (airlines, for example), or if something unfortunate happens that causes a big problem or disruption in your service. If this is the case, you will need to prioritize your responses to address the most serious problems first.

Prioritizing customer response is generally based on the perceived online influence of the customer. Logically, if a customer (such as a celebrity) has 65,000 social media followers, they have a lot more potential to damage your reputation by continuing to post negative comments than someone who has just 65 followers does. So, while you should ideally respond to both, if time and resources are tight you'll need to address the more influential customer first.

But how will you know how many online followers someone has? There are services such as Klout.com, Kred.com, PeerIndex.com, and Nuvi.com that rank people online based on their social media influence, and Facebook recently announced that they will start allowing advertisers to target top influencers.

12.13 INTEGRATE SOCIAL MEDIA TO THE ENTIRE CUSTOMER EXPERIENCE

Imagine that your favorite store just posted on Facebook "50% off all T-shirts today only." You drop what you're doing and rush down to the store, only to have the person working at the cash register charge you full price because they don't know anything about the Facebook sale. Disappointing, right? Customers don't care which department you work in; they want consistently high-quality service. All of the departments of your organization will need to be on board and fully-integrated with your social media strategy in order to provide a seamless, optimal customer experience from beginning to end.

There may likely be some overlap between your advertising and marketing departments; you should make sure that other forms of advertising (such as print, TV, or radio) align with your social media presence and include appropriate links. Your public relations and customer service departments need to be paying attention and responding to online complaints. Your staff should be aware of social media campaigns, and physical equipment (such as signage or receipts) should include links and invitations to share via social media. Your research-and-development department should listen to public input in designing new products. CEOs should interact with the public via social media, and your IT department should make sure that your website is optimized with the correct links, buttons, and apps.

12.14 ADMIT WHEN YOU SCREW UP, THEN LEVERAGE YOUR MISTAKES

Even the best of companies will occasionally make mistakes or encounter disasters. And, in the world of social media, it's inevitable that your customers will use the available platforms to comment, complain, and criticize. You might wish you could just ignore the whole issue, but sticking your head in the sand is definitely not an option. If you apologize promptly and take appropriate actions to right the situation, you may be able to win back your customers' support and trust, even actually improving your brand's reputation by dealing successfully with a setback.

Naturally, the first step is to acknowledge the problem and apologize. If possible, have a high-ranking person at your company make a brief statement on video. This helps put a human face to the problem, as long as the speaker is humble and sincere. You could also issue a written apology, but be sure to skip the legal jargon, keeping it friendly and genuine. Next, explain how you plan to fix the problem, or better yet, start fixing it immediately.

As we discussed earlier, in April 2009, two Domino's Pizza employees made a prank video about performing disgusting acts on the food. The video went viral, and Patrick Doyle, President of Domino's, posted a video in response on YouTube. The response was a little long, but the idea was

Domino's President Responds To Prank Video

An example of a crisis response video: Dominos Pizza CEO apologies for employees' bad behavior. *Source:* www.youtube.com[60]

good in terms of crisis communications. Watch the video at www.youtube .com/watch?v=dem6eA7-A2I. Along with this response, Domino's also made a series of videos about the company and how they were working on improving the flavor and quality of their product. In addition to showing behind-the-scenes content, these videos also helped distract people from finding the "Dirty Domino's Pizza" video when searching for "Domino's Pizza" on YouTube. It's been almost six years since the incident now, and the brand's reputation is finally starting to regain good standing.

Another good example is the clothing brand Loft, which got a lot of negative feedback for featuring an extremely tall and thin model in a catalog ad. Viewers commented that the pants were unflattering for "real women." The company apologized on Facebook, and began posting photos of actual Ann Taylor employees wearing the pants. The response online was overwhelmingly positive, because Loft had taken their customers' complaints seriously, taken action, and connected with them on a personal level.

 LOFT © All,

Thank you all so much for your comments and feedback. One of the requests we received was to show how regular women would wear these looks. Our Manager of Digital Programs (otherwise known as the woman who answers you on Facebook) has posted a gallery showing how she (me) would wears the pants at work, at night, and on the weekend. We hope you will take a look. And please stay tuned as we will be posting images of women at LOFT wearing the pants throughout the day!
June 17, 2010 at 9:01am · Like

Loft's response to complaints about how their pants don't look the same on real women as they do on the LOFT models. *Source:* www.facebook.com[61]

12.15 CONSISTENTLY DELIVER EXCITEMENT, SURPRISE, AND DELIGHT

With so many companies out there providing adequate—even great—products and services, what can you do to stand out from the competition? Well, how about making your clients smile? Delivering better-than-expected service? Amazing them with something unique? In other words, if you want to be a truly outstanding brand, you should make it your goal to deliver excitement, surprise, and delight.

Even seemingly small steps can have a big impact on your audience. For example, joining a conversation on Twitter to give some relevant information or provide a useful recommendation can really impress the person you have just helped. These little actions not only make people feel good, but also help build your brand's reputation. In a similar vein, some companies like to celebrate milestones with their fans, or randomly give away gifts to their followers.

Large campaigns can also deliver excitement, and major companies have had success with social media contests. For example, Franklin Sports had no more than 1,900 fans on its Facebook page until it launched a promotion to give away two playoff tickets to one lucky follower if the page reached 10,000 fans within two weeks. Baseball fans went crazy, recruiting all their friends to sign up. The enthusiasm was remarkable! Likewise, the New York City Department of Health certainly surprised followers on Twitter when it sent out tweets in the voice of a condom to promote safe sex.

12.16 DON'T OVER-PROMOTE; BUILD RELATIONSHIPS

Social media is generally not a place that welcomes aggressive marketing tactics and heavy-handed advertising. However, your fans are not naïve: they are aware that you are a business and that your goal is to sell products and make money, so they're generally willing to tolerate a certain amount of promotion. Some marketers have proposed the "80/20" rule, which states that approximately 80% of your content should *not* be traditional advertising: It should mainly consist of tips, advice, videos, links, funny pictures or any of the other forms of valuable content we have discussed so far. The remaining 20% of your content can fall into the category of direct advertising; customers do occasionally want to be informed of new items or sales, after all. Gary Vaynerchuck, or @GaryVee as he is known on Twitter, has written several books on social media; his most recent one is "Jab Jab Jab, Right Hook," which he has described as being the answer to the tendency of social media marketers for always giving and then forgetting to also occasionally ask for something. It is important to be giving and to promote other people, but it's also important to ask for something when appropriate.

You should be spending most of your time on social media working to build connections and earn the trust and loyalty of your online fans. Remember to LOVE (Listen, Offer, Visit and Engage). The book, *Likeable Social Media*[62] has suggested the following acronym as a guideline for conducting oneself on Twitter, but the advice holds true for most other forms of social media as well, and resembles the LOVE concept. The proposed acronym is TWEET:

T—Trust-building and building relationships.
W—Wisdom. Learn from industry leaders and your customers.
E—Ears open; you should be listening to the conversation.
E—Establish your brand, create a strong presence.
T—Teach the world about what you do.

12.17 LEARN WHAT GETS THE MOST ENGAGEMENT

There are many ways to improve engagement with your social media audience, as well as many ways to measure the variable level of engagement that different types of posts or content are generating. You should carefully consider how much time and resources you can realistically dedicate to engaging with your online consumers: can someone at your company accomplish that task, or do you need to hire someone dedicated specifically to building and maintaining your online community?

Next, consider what steps you can take to make your social media content more engaging. You should be an active listener and be genuinely interested in what your customers have to say. You should be taking all feedback seriously while doing your best to represent your company's core values; get your customers involved with your brand by building a community of people with shared interests and stimulating a conversation.

For instance, you can easily find out how many people have "liked" or commented on a post on Facebook, or how many followers have re-pinned your posts on Pinterest, and this information should give you a good idea of what kind of content your followers are attracted to. If you want more in-depth analysis of your social media content's reach, consider using some apps that help you track social media engagement; these include Bitly, Topsy, Twubs, Twitter Counter, and Social Mention. You can also use Google Analytics or the analytics tools that are provided for some business pages to examine which parts of your social media strategy are working best. If you need more information about engagement on Facebook, look at MeltWater's LikeAlyzer; if you just want a tool to track your amplification rate, applause rate, conversation rate, and economic value, look at True Social Metrics. New measurement tools and dashboards are being introduced all the time. Nuvi is a good solution if you need to track more than 50,000 mentions per month. SaleForce Marketing Cloud and Sprinklr are enterprise-level solutions.

12.18 IT'S A MARATHON

Success and a multitude of followers cannot be achieved overnight on social media platforms. It is unlikely that you will see immediate and tangible results from your social media efforts; yet, in the long run, steps like increasing brand awareness or improving customer service will really pay off. Many companies jump into social media only to quit shortly afterwards just because they did not see huge numbers in their first week of engagement. Remember that, just like in real life, building a friendship or a relationship is a long, slow, cumulative process, and you'll need to devote significant time—months or even years—in order to reach that level of connection.

In many ways, social media marketing is a game of quality, not quantity. Sure, there are billions of people on the Internet, but you can't connect with all of them, nor should that be your goal. Many people tend to obsess over numbers, statistics, metrics of reach or influence, but it is probably more fruitful to focus on building strong connections with a loyal following of people who really care about what you do. There is no doubt that having 100 engaged and loyal followers is better than having 100,000 random spam-bots who "like" you. There are a lot of "get followers fast" schemes out there, promising to help you gain fans quickly, but these are usually not worth pursuing.

12.19 PLAN AHEAD: MAKE A SOCIAL MEDIA CONTENT CALENDAR

As we saw in section 12.5, consistency is key in social media; you'll need to post regularly to maintain the interest of your audience. In fact, when companies suddenly stop posting on social media, or only post sporadically, they may give the impression that their page has been abandoned. If this happens, people will begin to wonder what exactly is going on at your company, or may even think that you've gone out of business. The problem, of course, is that it's also really challenging to come up with good quality content to post week after week after week. A great suggestion to help you overcome this problem and manage your social media schedule would be to create a calendar that will help you plan out posts in advance.

With a social media content calendar, you can map out a strategy in advance, and fill in any blanks as needed. Thus, you may want to build in seasonal themes as well as promotions around the big holidays. Maybe there are also other dates that are significant in your industry, such as regional holidays, special events, conferences, and so on. Additionally, you should also try to anticipate the times when fans are likely to be searching online for deals, discounts, information, or stories, and plan ahead accordingly.

Of course it's always a good idea to also be spontaneous: Some posts will just occur naturally as things develop. But creating a social media

DATE	1	2	3	4	5	6
DAY	SUN	MON	TUES	WED	THURS	FRI
TOPIC	TULIPS	GROUNDHOG DAY	TUTORIAL	WICKED	#TBT	INSIDER
AUDIENCE	35–54	ALL	ALL	ALL	20–35	ALL
OWNER	SB	CH	SB	SB	JP	CH
FACEBOOK	IMAGE POST	CUTE PHOTO		TBT PHOTO		VIDEO
TWITTER	TEXT	PHOTO		TEXT		TEXT
PINTEREST	NEW BOARD			BOARD	PIN 10	
GOOGLE+	IMAGE POST	PHOTO	HOW TO		PHOTO	VIDEO
YOUTUBE			TUTORIAL	VIDEO		VIDEO

calendar can help you distribute your content evenly and identify problem areas or time periods in which you'll need to come up with more, or more interesting, material. This will also enable you to be ahead of the game, and well-prepared for those special holidays and events.

Your calendar could look like the one above and it could be built out to include all copy—the text for each post as well as deadlines and instructions for where to get various resources.

12.20 ADD SOCIAL ICONS AND "LIKE" BUTTONS TO FACILITATE SHARING

Without question, the Facebook "like" button, which was introduced in April 2010, has become an indispensable and extremely influential part of the social media experience. It has been added to over 3 million websites already, and it allows users to instantly express their approval and support of individuals, statements, companies, brands, articles, and every other type of content. Perhaps even more importantly, the "like" button has been a key factor in the personalization of the online experience:

Seeing what your friends "like" is a powerful recommendation. We are all highly likely to judge companies and products based on the "likes" of our real-world friends and acquaintances. The "like" feature helps companies build their reputation and gain the trust of followers.

Because the number of "likes," retweets, +1's, etc. that an item receives highly correlates to its prominence in feeds and/or in search results, you really do want to make sure that the ability to share items on the most appropriate platforms is accessible and readily visible on all of your pages and other content. The appropriate buttons should not only be added to individual blog posts, but to blog author pages or profiles as well. They should also be found on landing pages, home pages, thank-you pages (which customers typically see after they have completed an online purchase), and email newsletters, among other places.

Mashable does a good job of making sharing buttons easy to see and use. They also post the overall number of shares for each post, a good measure of the social proof of the post. The more interesting the post, the more shares it usually achieves in the social media universe.

A post from Mashable.com showing effective use of sharing icons for each of the major social networks.
Source: www.mashable.com[63]

12.21 TWEET YOUR JOB APPLICATION AND GET LINKEDIN TO YOUR CAREER

Social media has become an invaluable resource for just about everything people need to do, buy, or learn in life. It is especially useful in networking situations: those times when you call on your community of friends, acquaintances, and colleagues to help you out. But did you know that Twitter can even help you land a job?

There are many creative strategies for finding employment via Twitter—one easy way is to tweet like an industry expert. Your tweets will showcase your knowledge and what you have to say, and, if you present yourself like the professional and expert that you surely are, employers may be impressed and seek you out. Moreover, you can use hashtags to find job opportunities and respond to them; you can also use Twitter to get into contact with recruiters and employees at a company you may want to work for. Taking it one step further, you could build a network of people in your field, so that you'll be among the first to know about opportunities when they open up. Last but not least, remember that all those people on Twitter exist in the real world too—so you might use Twitter as a tool to set up a face-to-face meeting and/or organize a tweetup, which is a meeting of people who tweet around similar topics.

Similarly, LinkedIn is fast replacing your need for a résumé, as recruiters are often scaling LinkedIn before posting openings. Start building your LinkedIn network early and you will soon start realizing its value, as your LinkedIn contacts will connect you with opportunities, share knowledge, and help you further build your network. Connecting on LinkedIn doesn't just need to take place only on the platform, either. Peter Kuperman had a creative strategy: He would use LinkedIn's InMail feature to invite people with similar interests to dinner at his apartment in San Francisco; he held one such dinner a month for 10–20 people each time. The dinners were organized around different themes; for example, one month the theme might be green buildings, while on another month it might be opera. Each dinner would have a guest speaker; all the guests

Peter Kuperman's *Chef by Night Dinner Parties*

Peter Kuperman's Chef by Night Dinners allow him to connect with potential customers in person after he has invited them to his house through LinkedIn. *Source:* www.peterkuperman.com[64]

had to do was bring some wine and help prepare the meal. Then, at the end of the year, Peter invited all his dinner attendees to a big cocktail party, where he could ask people to consider his services as a hedge fund manager. Since hedge fund managers are not allowed to advertise, this was a great way to build his network, make friends, and be able to promote his business all at the same time.

CHAPTER 13

ALL THE BEST TIPS YOU'LL EVER NEED FOR THE TOP SOCIAL NETWORKS TODAY

13.1 FACEBOOK

With more than 1.3 billion monthly active users, Facebook is the most visited social network in the world; members of your target audience will almost definitely be using it. Facebook has become a powerful tool used all over the world for communication, news, business, advertising, organizing, and much more. Engaging with your fans through Facebook will be a key component of any successful social media marketing strategy. Facebook offers a variety of features and options suited to different types of businesses (to be discussed in more detail below), and even though the tools and rules of Facebook are constantly changing, there is one constant: On Facebook, like on all social media, the best way to reach your audience is not by breeding hype or aggressively trying to sell something, but by creating high-quality content that users will be interested in reading, viewing, and hopefully sharing with their friends.

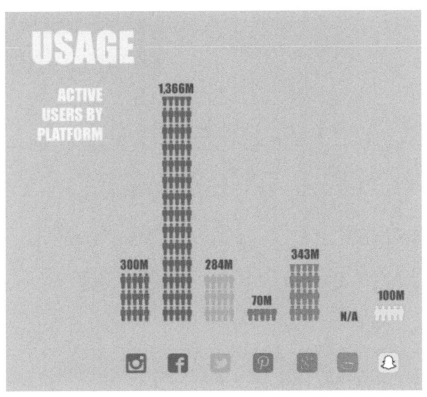

USAGE

ACTIVE USERS BY PLATFORM

1,366M

300M   284M   343M   100M

70M   N/A

Number of active monthly users by platform as of February 2015. *Source:* www.digitalinformationworld.com[65]

Let's begin by looking at Facebook company pages, which are also sometimes called business timelines or business pages. Company pages are used for the official representation of a company, but may also be used by other entities, such as governments, celebrities and public figures, and nonprofit organizations. There are a couple of significant differences between personal profiles and company pages: Most importantly, a company page's connection to the viewer is one-way. When a fan "likes" a company, they are able to view the company's public posts and photos, but the company is not able to view the fan's personal content. Company pages also provide a variety of analytical tools and features, which we will discuss below.

In general, when creating a company page, you should follow the same standards you would use in creating any professional material. Choose a good name for your page; it's not possible to change your name after you have two hundred or more followers, so choose carefully! A customized URL (also called a vanity URL) is helpful, because it will make it easier for people to find your page. The cover photo that you use will appear every time that you post or that your company is "liked"; this is going to be one of the main images associated with your company on Facebook, so make sure that you upload a great photo, in the correct format. Your photo should be recognizable at a small size, and the caption should provide an apt description, or possibly a link or call-to-action offer.

Facebook cover photo dimensions for your business page. *Source:* Suse Barnes

Make sure you provide accurate and up-to-date information about your business, including your address, operating hours, phone number or email, type of business, etc. Providing an accurate description with appropriate key words will make it much easier for people to find your business in an online search.

If you install custom app tabs (which will appear along the left side of the screen), bear in mind that they can usually be customized; this is much more attractive than the generic format that they often appear in. It's a good idea to customize them to match the colors of your brand or the overall look of your page; you can also rearrange the order of the tabs that appear below your cover photo (typically, "about," "timeline," "photos," and so on). You may also want to change one of those so that it links to calls to action, special offers, or product information—

for example, the retailer Target has a customized tab for product recalls. Whichever tab is positioned directly below your profile picture is going to be the most noticeable.

Target's customized tab icons on Facebook. *Source:* www.facebook.com[66]

There are several ways to use Facebook's geolocation technology to benefit your business: First of all, mobile users can locate your business and see if any of their friends have checked in there or made recommendations. Reviews and check-ins generate status updates which feature the business's name, profile photo, and star rating, and such updates are seen by the customer-reviewer's friends. Reviews and check-ins will also make your business rank higher in feeds and searches. Currently, reviews are only possible for businesses with a physical location—that, however, may change in the future. In order to receive the benefits of reviews, you need to have your Facebook page also set up as a Place page—essentially, this feature locates you on a map. Also keep in mind that if you don't have a Place page set up, it is possible that when someone tries to check-in to your business they may inadvertently create a Place name for you, which will not be linked to your actual business; that would result in valuable reviews and check-ins not being associated correctly with your business, and you'd be wasting any positive feedback received. Once you do have your Place page established, make sure you remind your followers to check-in and share with their friends!

Facebook has many other handy tools which you'll want to learn to use well. Probably the most important among these are the "like" and "share" buttons, which you should make sure are clearly displayed near blog posts, products, photos, etc. You can also "pin" or "highlight" an important post so that it stays at the top of your timeline for up to a week, where it will be most visible to fans. Additionally, you can embed posts from a personal profile or company page to other sites, such as a blog post or email newsletter—this can make repurposing content across platforms really easy! It is okay to repost your best content from time to time, but don't overdo it; Facebook penalizes companies that repeatedly copy and paste the same content.

Remember that you want to avoid what is known as "click-baiting," in other words, posting low-quality material with a tantalizing or misleading title. These types of post get a lot of "clicks," but people are usually disappointed with the content and don't bother to share it further. On the other hand, due to changes in Facebook's algorithms, posts that are especially high-quality (receiving a lot of "likes" or comments, indicating high levels of viewer engagement) may be repeatedly pushed back to the top of your fans' newsfeed, so more people will end up viewing it.

A well-designed page will provide you with literally hundreds of ways you can connect with your audience and potential customers: You can encourage your customers to "check-in," leave a review, give feedback, and "like," share or comment on your best content. Make sure that you extend these requests using appropriate language, and that you don't do so too often—you don't want to seem desperate. A friendly and direct call to action is usually the best route. Keep your posts timely, and respond to comments and questions promptly. Use hashtags to encourage conversations. You can offer your viewers promotions, contests, or special events, and thank your fans for their support. Many company pages recognize milestones and achievements, either within the company (posting a photo of the employee of the month, or announcing the company's great new location), or those of their customers ("Longtime customer José celebrated his birthday at our restaurant!").

You may want to go a step further and consider cross-promoting with other Facebook pages/companies that offer complementary goods or services. For example, a local gym could partner with a sporting goods retailer; they would "like" each other's pages and post about the other business from time to time, recommending them to their own followers and fans. Your Facebook page can also be used for doing research on your audience, either by examining the results and reactions you get to a variety of content, or by directly asking your followers to answer questionnaires or surveys.

Company pages have a variety of features and useful analytical tools for businesses. For example, you can track the growth of your page and which types of posts your audience prefers, get demographic information about your audience, and even keep tabs on your competitors. Such information should help you understand your audience better, so that you can further tailor your content to their needs. Company pages can also buy advertising in a variety of ways, something that is not an option on personal profiles. For example, purchasing a "boost" will increase the visibility of your post for a few days; the cost depends on the number of viewers your post will reach. A company can also create and pay for a customized advertisement, determining the layout, location, target, and timing (for more information on advertising, see www.facebook.com /business/products/ads).

Individuals have personal profiles on Facebook, which can be used to present who you are, connect with your friends, and share information and interests. It's important to know that using a personal profile for commercial purposes is not allowed on Facebook, and any Facebook account used inappropriately can be shut down. If you intend to use Facebook for business purposes, you should either create a separate company page or convert your personal profile to a company page. However, a personal profile can still be used in several strategic yet non-commercial ways to support your business, as discussed in more detail in chapter 7.

Of course, Facebook can work in tandem with all of the other forms of social media we have discussed, and vice versa. Did the CEO of your company write an excellent blog post? Share it on Facebook! Are there great photos of your newest design on Instagram? Share it on Facebook! And make sure to include the Facebook "like" and "share" buttons next to products on your website, interesting articles, or blog posts, etc., so that viewers can help spread the word. Finally, keep in mind that new features and new rules are constantly being added and updated on Facebook, therefore you'll need to keep abreast of developments by regularly researching the relevant information on new features and legal limitations.

FACEBOOK ACTION STEPS

1. Create a Page at www.facebook.com/pages/create. Choose the type of business that best describes you, and follow the step-by-step instructions.

2. Add a Cover Photo. Currently the dimensions for these are 851 × 314 pixels, at 72 pixels per inch. If you save your image as a JPG or PNG, these will be sized appropriately.

3. Build your content calendar outside of Facebook, so that you know what you're going to be posting and when.

4. Add your first post.

5. Add one post per day for a week.

6. Ask all of your friends to like your page and share it with their friends.

7. Make sure you listen carefully and remain attuned to what your audience wants from your page.

8. Look at www.likealyzer.com to get an idea of things you could improve about your page.

9. Consider boosting a post.

10. Visit other pages and "like" them from your business page.

11. Continue posting regularly.

12. Post a question to your audience.

13. Learn what is working and what is not by reviewing your Facebook Insights and any advertising reports you may receive in the Ads Manager.

14. Consider promoting your page to get more page "likes."

15. Engage with your fans by asking questions, responding to comments, "liking" comments, "liking" other pages, and saying "thank you."

16. Remember to LOVE: Listen, Offer, Visit, and Engage—and, most of all, try to have fun doing it.

13.2 TWITTER

Twitter may be best known as a way to post messages of 140 characters or less, but it has a variety of other uses as well; it can be used to monitor conversations, interact with customers and manage customer service issues, share content, and promote offers, among other things.

Once more, remember that the basic features of Twitter are as follows: A tweet is a short message that goes out to anyone following you. It may consist of text (140 characters or less), an image, a link, or a combination of these. Other users are free to "retweet" (i.e., share) any post of their choosing by someone that they follow; followers can also use the "favorite" button to show support or approval of a post. The @reply feature lets a user send a message to one or more specific Twitter users; only the recipient and anyone who follows both the sender and the recipient will see it. A direct message (or DM) is a private message between two accounts. But perhaps the most well-known contribution of Twitter to the world of social media is the use of the hashtag (#). Hashtags are used to group tweets of the same kind together, and can be used by one individual or multiple users. Their use has proven so effective that they have been adopted by other types of social media, and are now also used on Facebook and Instagram, among others.

If you're setting up a Twitter account for your company, the first step is to choose your username, which should be short and clear. If possible, it is much preferable to use your company name and/or your own name, rather than making up a random name or using a name with numbers in it, à la AOL: for example, it's much easier to remember @susby than it is to remember @susby4278.[67] Complete your bio accurately; this information appears in search results for your company. Upload a profile picture—this could be a photo of you (your smiling face, please) or a brand logo. Do not use a photo of your cat, and remember that profiles without photos are suspected of being fake accounts. You also have the option of creating a custom Twitter header along with customized background images.

Many companies are now using Twitter for customer service, and customers expect a prompt reply (often within 30 minutes or less!) when they tweet a complaint. If you're not available 24/7, you should let your customers know in your bio or on your cover page exactly during which hours your customer service department is available, or by when they can expect a response to their queries.

Because Twitter posts are short, a typical user might tweet three times a day or more, whereas that frequency of activity would be considered annoying on another form of social media. Therefore, while you might share an occasional tweet on other social media such as Facebook, you probably don't want to repost every single tweet—such a practice would come across as obnoxious and spammy. Similarly, posting more than two or three tweets in an hour can cause people to tune out (unless you have a very large following), so don't overdo it—go for quality over quantity! Consider the tips discussed previously for the best types of content to post; in general, selfless and engaging (not direct advertising) material works best. One way to discover which of your tweets are most popular is by using a tool such as My Top Tweet.

Due to the 140 character limit, spelling, punctuation, and grammar have an even bigger impact on Twitter than elsewhere; take care to craft your tweets well. Also, if you exceed the limit, your post will spill over into multiple tweets, which makes them confusing and frustrating for your followers to read. If you really must exceed the limit, consider using a service such as TwitLonger, which will allow you to type longer messages by posting only part of the message on Twitter, along with a link making it easy for your followers to continue reading the full message elsewhere. If several people at your company are using the same Twitter account, make sure that they sign off with their initials so that it's clear who authored each tweet: Look at www.twitter.com/HiltonSuggests for an example. You can occasionally post the same content under different titles, as not everyone among your followers will have seen each tweet— in fact, this can be a great way to test which timing and which titles get the most engagement. There are also third-party apps and services that you can use to schedule and automatically post tweets.

Use hashtags to group tweets, drive engagement, strengthen your brand identity, join conversations, and gather feedback. It's generally not recommended to use more than one or two hashtags per tweet, but keep in mind that tweets which include hashtags typically receive twice as much engagement as those with no hashtags. Make your hashtags easy to read by capitalizing words and avoiding symbols. (Example: #GreatPromotion is easier to read than #greatpromotion.) You may want to create a custom hashtag which you use regularly that reflects the name of your company, or specialized hashtags for events or special promotions. For example, if your restaurant is called Leo's Bar and Grill, you could use #LeosBar; your customers could also use that hashtag when they post about your business: "Leo's Bar has the best margaritas! #LeosBar #SaturdayNight." This is also a great way to collect feedback; if you search the #LeosBar hashtag, you will easily see what your fans (or critics) are saying about you. This gives you a chance to reach out to your loyal customers, as well as tactfully engage or offer help if someone has had a bad experience.

There are many other ways to connect with your fans and drive engagement. It's a good idea to find a balance between tweets, replies, and retweets, without over-promoting yourself. Respond to @mentions and direct messages promptly, and show appreciation to your followers by clicking the star icon to "favorite" their tweets, or by following them back. Tweets can also include photos, which are typically popular content—these, however, sometimes don't display completely. Similarly to other forms of social media, you can use Twitter to share special offers or deals with your customers, or create games and contests. Vine is Twitter's answer to Instagram video—we'll take a look at Vine in section 13.8. Finally, similarly to Facebook, you can "pin" important tweets, keeping them at the top of your feed for extra visibility.

The best way to grow your following is to follow people that seem interesting to you, and also follow people who are likely to follow you back. When you first start using Twitter, it may be tempting to just follow all the celebrities—but in fact you'll get more out of it if you search for a topic that interests you and then start listening to what people are tweeting about around that topic. A study by Dan Zarrella found that tweeting 22 times per day was the sweet spot in order to grow your Twitter following; remember that no one is on Twitter all day, and when they are they are mostly just looking at their home Twitter feed. For this reason, the frequency of your tweets is important. Just like radio advertising, the more you tweet, the more visible and top-of-mind you become, and the more likely it will be that people will want to follow you.

Twitter can also be used for company research: You can use the "search" feature to find and connect with people who have tweeted about your business or industry. This is an important tool for finding out how the public feels about your company, as you can easily see what kind of negative feedback about you is out there. As mentioned above, Twitter is increasingly used for customer service; if that is the case with your business, you may want to consider creating a separate Twitter profile dedicated exclusively to that purpose. You can also consider using direct messages or a personal profile to deal with especially pressing or private issues. Similarly to Facebook, a variety of analytical tools are available to companies on Twitter, enabling them, for instance, to measure how many people clicked on something that they posted, or how many retweeted an item. Finally, paid advertising is also available on Twitter.

A BREAKDOWN OF TWITTER

This is the home screen and this is where you will see all the posts of the people you are following. There are several elements to be aware of on this page (top left going right):

An example of the Twitter home screen. *Source:* www.twitter.com

1. Notifications is where you will find your news, including people who have followed you or mentioned you.

2. Messages is where your DM (direct messages) are stored.

3. #Discover will help you find new people to follow.

4. The search box is where you should enter a keyword term or hashtag to find out what people are saying around each.

5. The little photo of you to the right of the search bar is where you will find all your Twitter settings.

6. The little blue square next to the profile photo is the "compose a tweet" button. You can also just enter something in the "What's Happening?" field.

7. Under the "What's Happening?" field you can see a Promoted Post: that is the beginning of the stream. Since this screenshots indicates that I'm following 1,881 people, the stream is where any tweets made by those people will show up.

8. Under the Sponsored post (image), you see Ramzi M.Rihani with his handle or Twitter ID, @ramzirihani after it.

9. @ramzirihani's tweet includes two hashtags and two @replies. Can you identify each one?

Below each tweet on the Twitter interface, you'll see the following icons:

Reply   Retweet   Buffer   Favorite   Hootsuite

Icons below each tweet with different functions. *Source:* www.twitter.com[68]

Buffer and Hootsuite enable you to store retweets in a queue for sending at a later time.

ACTION STEPS FOR TWITTER

1. Sign up for an account using your name or your company name.

2. Search for some topics that interest you in the search bar.

3. "Follow" 5 people.

4. Listen to the stream.

5. The next day, follow 5 more people and listen. Are you seeing anything interesting? Do certain profiles stick out as being more engaging that others? You'll soon start to see a pattern and you'll be able to find the right people to follow.

6. Repeat steps 3 through 5 a few times, and then you'll be ready to start tweeting.

7. Send your first tweet. Say something like "Hello Twitterverse, we're looking forward to joining the [insert you industry] conversation."

8. Start retweeting and favoriting tweets that you appreciate and that you would want your followers to see.

9. Twitter is knowledge-sharing, so if you see anything that is particularly useful to your industry or may help others in their careers, tweet a link to it.

10. Consider using a URL shortening and scheduling tool like HootSuite.

11. Remember that you need to tweet a lot more than you post on Facebook, so scheduling your tweets will save you time. Refer to the social media editorial calendar that you created in the Facebook action steps in order to know what to tweet about.

12. You don't have to be on Twitter all day, but if you see any mentions or conversations that seem interesting, that would be a good time to join in the discussion.

Happy tweeting!

13.3 GOOGLE+

When it was first launched in 2011, Google+ was considered by many as a potential new alternative to Facebook. With approximately 540 million active users, Google+ cannot compare to the sheer size and dominance of Facebook in terms of popularity; however, it has several interesting features that are not available anywhere else, and this makes it a crucial tool in the online world. Because it is linked to Google's other products (News, Maps, Docs, Gmail), not to mention their search engine, Google basically dominates the field of web searches—consequently, if you want to be found online, you should start by creating a Google+ profile.

You'll need to begin by setting up a business page, not a personal profile. (Similar to Facebook, these are distinct categories with different functions and uses). Go to www.google.com/business to start. You can get a custom URL, which will make it easy for people to find you; once you choose the URL you can't change it, so make sure you pick a really pertinent one. Choose a cover photo and a profile photo; as with Facebook, make sure the photos are appropriate, attractive, and correctly formatted. Create a tagline, which is a brief summary of what your business is, and complete the "about" section with relevant keywords and links. The more accurately you describe your business, the more likely the right customers will be to find it in an online search. While Facebook uses "likes," Google uses the "+1" feature to show liking, agreement, or support. By adding the +1 button to posts, viewers can easily share your content. Your Google+ page can also be linked to a "Local Places" page if you have a physical location; Local Places pages include reviews and photos of a business, and can be especially helpful for mobile users who are trying to find you while on the road.

In terms of managing your networks, Google+'s "Circles" feature is quite interesting: it enables users to assign their Google+ contacts to separate Circles, so they can then distribute specific content to selected Circles. For example, a business could create Circles for "VIP customers," "potential clients," and "current partners," sending each of them content tailored to their particular needs and interests, exclusive offers, or relevant information. Furthermore, you can use Circles to dialogue with people in your industry, or have fans/customers/clients circle your page on

Google+ so that they can stay up-to-date with your developments. If you manage your Circles well, you can really microtarget specific audiences with content perfectly tailored to them. An interesting point to keep in mind is that individual members will not be able to see which Circle you have placed them in—the categories you create remain private. Also, you cannot put yourself into someone's circle; they themselves will have to choose to add you to one of their circles.

When you post content on Google+ it is immediately indexed, which makes it available to a wider audience via search engines. The first sentence of whatever you post will compose part of the title tag that comes up in search results, which can affect ranking— so make sure you write that first sentence with care. Due to Google's personalization, your content is more likely to show up in your contacts' online searches as well. You also have the option to embed your Google+ posts on other sites (such as a blog), so you can easily repurpose and share your content; additionally, posts can be edited and reformatted even after you have made them. Pictures and videos can increase engagement, as well as @mentions of your followers; so can the use of hashtags.

Although Google+ has strict terms about the kinds of contests or promotions you can run on it, with a little bit of creativity you can still engage your audience without violating the rules. For example, by offering a sneak preview of a product as an incentive, you could ask fans to suggest ideas and you can then select the one you like best; or you could ask them to share pictures of themselves using your product, and you could showcase these on your page. In this case, their reward in lieu of a prize would be being featured on your company's page.

As with Twitter, you can use a variety of search techniques on Google+ to find potential customers or discover people who are talking about your brand or product and address their concerns. Try entering keywords or hashtags that are related to your brand, and then filter your content by type. You can use the Circles feature to organize your results, sorting people you find into separate categories such as "loyal fans" or "dissatisfied customers," and then interact with them accordingly—remember that they can't see which Circle you've put them in! Another interesting feature is that, once you've identified a person that is of interest to you—perhaps a potential client or brand ambassador—you can use a tool called "View Ripples," which allows you to measure the "virality" of posts; that is, it enables you to see the magnitude of an individual's circle of influence. Once you have identified potential followers that you may want to contact, it's easy to email them using Google+. However, use this approach with caution—people can be easily put off by unsolicited marketing emails.

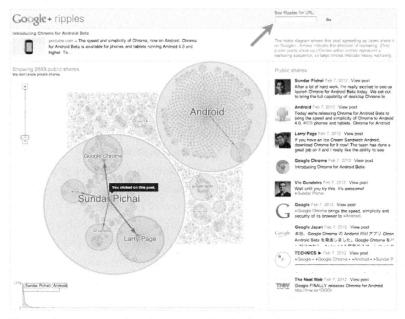

Ripples on Google+ show how far each post is spread based on the number of people in each network of people interacting with the post. *Source:* www.plus.google.com[69]

Still other ways to connect include Google+ "Communities" and "Hangouts." The Communities feature allows your followers to gather and discuss your business, and you can interact with them as well. Conversely, you could join a community for your niche, sector, industry, or field to make connections and share knowledge with your colleagues. Hangouts is a way for up to 10 people to join a free video-conference. There is a variety of creative uses for Google Hangouts: imagine collaborating with colleagues in different cities or countries, or having a convenient consultation with your clients, no matter where they are located. This is a huge asset for any business or project that would benefit from face-to-face communication or requires group discussions. Furthermore, Google Hangouts are automatically recorded and can be posted on YouTube if you choose to do so—this way, you could easily use the Hangouts feature to give a demo, presentation, conference, or workshop, and then share the video on your Googl+ profile or other social media. And, as discussed above, because your video is already in the Google system it will be easily locatable by anyone searching for it. If you're in a Hangout that you want to broadcast, make sure you're using Hangouts On Air, because the regular Hangouts feature doesn't include the broadcasting feature.

Because it's important to reply to likes or comments promptly, you might want to use Notification Count, which is a Chrome extension that displays how many new notifications you have. Another Chrome extension called Extend Share lets you easily share Google+ posts on Facebook, LinkedIn, and Twitter; and to help you determine which social media strategy is working best, you can use Google Analytics. Paid advertising is available on Google+ for pages with 1,000 or more followers.

ACTIONS STEPS FOR GOOGLE+

1. Make sure you have a Google account so that you can create a Google+ profile and page.
2. Start your business page at www.google.com/business.
3. Add your profile photos and cover photo. These should not be the same image as was used on Facebook.
4. Start building your circles and adding people to them.
5. Start posting content to Google+ as planned in your editorial calendar.
6. "+1" other people's posts, and comment on any that you find interesting.
7. Come back tomorrow and repeat the same process until you have more people following you than you could ever have imagined, and your search results are creating hot leads.

13.4 PINTEREST

Pinterest can be described as an "online scrapbook" or "virtual bulletin board" where users can collect and organize images from around the web that intrigue or interest them. As the name implies, it's a place where you can pin your interest for future reference—and since it's social, you can easily share your interests with other Pinterest users (called pinners). According to R. J. Moore in his blog, RJMetrics, Pinterest has over 40 million active users, 80% of whom are women; even more remarkably, 92% of all people pinning are women.[70]

As with other social media platforms, Pinterest users connect with their friends or a larger online community, and also follow inspirational people and brands they like. Personal/individual pages are separate from business pages. Pinterest is currently one of the top five social media sites; moreover, among social media sites, it is the second largest driver of web traffic. That means that while Pinterest itself is not a retail site, millions of people click through it to check out other websites, and therefore often end up ultimately buying things that they originally saw on Pinterest. In short, Pinterest users have buyer intent: They are looking for things to buy.

You should sign up for Pinterest as a business, or if you had already signed up as an individual, you can easily convert your account. Having a business account gives you access to a variety of tools, case studies, and links to buttons that you can use on your website. In order to sign up you will need to choose a username and URL; the obvious choice may be to use your company name, but you could also use another word combination or a slogan. Complete the "about" section thoroughly yet briefly, using relevant keywords. Add your website and verify it. (Verification shows that you are a trusted source of information). Upload your properly formatted profile image—this is usually the image of a figurehead or a company logo.

Once you have created your profile, you can start exploring some of the following content and marketing strategies: To begin with, you need to pin good images, properly formatted to look sharp. There is no limit on the vertical size of images on Pinterest, but the maximum horizontal width is 735 pixels. Make sure that your website, blog, or other online content has a "pin it" button, making it easy for anyone who likes what they see to pin your item to their Pinterest board. This consideration goes hand in hand with the notion that you should make sure you provide highly attractive, "pinnable" visual images on your website or other media: You may have a great web store, but if it's mostly text or the pictures are just mediocre, people will likely not be inspired to "pin" it. Also, Pinterest only lets users pin from webpages where there is at least one image. Because Pinterest is a such a highly visual site, focusing on the quality of your images can increase your success. Lastly, be aware of trends in colors, fonts, and styles, as some tend to perform better than others.

You'll need to pin consistently: if possible, as much as a few times a day. Approximately 80% of the content on Pinterest consists of re-pinned posts, so by adding your own, original posts you are really adding new, quality content. Of course, it's also a good idea to pin content from other sources, as long as the images are high-quality, interesting, inspirational, or helpful—this can help your page develop into a great resource. You'll have several boards reflecting different niches or themes; try to keep the boards' names simple and clear enough to be found easily in a search. You may want to use very specific names to differentiate your boards from the thousands of others on Pinterest. For each board you can select which image will be the cover and position it accordingly. You can also rearrange the order and location of your boards, allowing you to position important or interesting boards more prominently. For each pin you can provide a description, and here too you should take care to describe the image or item accurately, using distinct keywords. Finally, you can create "secret" boards, visible only to you until you decide to make them public—these can be really effective for seasonal campaigns or for offering sneak peeks to selected followers.

There are many interesting ways in which you can use Pinterest as a business. One new feature, which makes pins more useful and engaging, is called "Rich Pins." Rich Pins allow you to share more information, such as the price and availability of a product, maps, or other details on top of the relevant pins. The information displayed on Rich Pins is updated automatically by lifting data from your website, making Rich Pins especially easy for followers to shop from Pinterest. Additionally, you can get a lot of insight about your consumers' likes, wants, and preferences by examining your followers' boards.

Another popular option for companies on Pinterest has to do with making special incentives or other offers accessible to your followers: Sports brands often offer workout tips, packaged as sleek infographics or including other with attractive images; food companies offer seasonal recipes. You may also ask your followers to participate in a contest, game, or challenge—this can even be a great way to crowdsource photos: Your followers will provide great, authentic content! To give one more example: A furniture company could create a special Pinterest board titled "Show us your sofa!" Real-life customers could pin photos of themselves, their family, and their living room, and tag the furniture company, which could then share their photos on the special board. Other fun ideas include VIP boards, guest pinners, meet the team, company history, sneak peeks of upcoming products, tutorials and how-to boards, and reviews and recommendations boards. Well-designed infographics can be helpful too, in case your product or business does not exactly lend itself to being photographed well.

ACTION STEPS FOR PINTEREST

1. Sign up for an account at www.pinterest.com.
2. Search for pins related to your industry, business, hobbies, and interests.
3. Search for your competition to see what they have been doing on Pinterest so far.
4. Start building boards by pinning photos and images that you like from the search results you achieved.
5. Pin every day for two weeks.
6. Consider converting your personal account to a business Pinterest account so that you can start looking at analytics (http://analytics.pinterest.com).
7. Make sure your website images are easy to pin and look good when pinned.
8. Describe each image with relevant keywords and hashtags so that each image can be easily found when people are searching for similar keyword terms.

9. Verify your website so that it shows up as verified when people are viewing images pinned from your site.

10. Be creative. Take a look at Uniqlo's pinstorm video. They were able to take over Pinterest for a time by having several people posting many strategic images.

Uniqlo used create a Pinstorm on Pinterest by getting a team of people to post images all at the same time. This was effectively a Pinterest takeover for a short period of time, which resulted in a lot of earned media for the brand. *Source:* www.youtube.com[71]

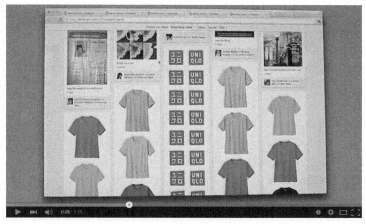

Another frame from the Uniqlo Dry Mesh Project video about how they created a Pinstorm. *Source:* www.youtube.com[72]

11. Don't post only about your business and products. Post about things your audience is interested in. Chobani Greek yogurt does a great job of this. They show fitness boards and lifestyle boards in addition to the expected recipe and nutrition boards; see http://www.pinterest.com /Chobani.

12. Consider organizing contests in order to grow your boards and followers.

13. Consider working with an analytics company like Piqora, Curalate, or Tailwind to get more detailed analysis of pins and the economic value you can earn from strategically managing your Pinterest account.

13.5 LINKEDIN

LinkedIn is the world's largest professional social network, with 347 million users worldwide as of February 2015. It is used for job seeking and recruitment, retention, industry collaboration, and business-to-business connections. It's a place where professionals can get down to business, so to speak. In fact, some professionals may have a LinkedIn profile even if they do not have a Facebook profile; therefore you might be able to reach people on LinkedIn who would not be available through other social media channels.

A LinkedIn Company Page is ideal for sharing products and services, cultivating professional connections, following industry news, recruiting, and providing information about business. To set up your Company Page, fill out all of the sections completely and accurately, including details about your location, size, contact information, industry, and so on. (It's a good idea to create both a personal profile for yourself individually, as well as a page for your company; here we will focus mainly on the company pages, but much of the same advice holds true for personal profiles.) It's important to note that in order to add a company page you must have a company email address; you cannot create a company page with a Gmail or Outlook email address. Once you've created your page, add a profile photo, logo, and banner images. Interestingly, on LinkedIn some people choose *not* to include a personal photo, even though it's recommended to do so. If you're using a photo, it should be

professional-looking, not a snapshot of you at a party. If your page
(or profile) contains quite a lot of text, you can use bullet points to make
it more readable. You'll want to include a summary of your company
that puts your brand in a good light, showcases your assets, and explains
what makes you unique. Optimize your text with concise, accurate
descriptions and relevant keywords to make sure you rank highly in
Google and LinkedIn searches; you should use both broad terms and
specific, detailed terms.

Company profiles basically provide an overview of what a business
does or what their products are. They also often include information
about any open positions at the company, and enable you to view their
employees who have LinkedIn accounts. A dynamic LinkedIn page is
quite useful from a recruitment perspective, as it can draw the most
talented people in your industry to work for your company. As much as
possible, you should encourage all of your employees to get on LinkedIn
as well, by creating personal profiles and adding you as an employer;
this helps create a larger network, which increases your standing and
influence.

LinkedIn is also a great tool for business-to-business connections;
this is a space that's much more conducive to professional communication than Facebook. On LinkedIn it is also possible to create groups for
people in your industry to connect and collaborate; if your business is
an architecture firm, for example, you might create a group where local
architects can discuss new ideas and developments in their field. By
using the tools available on LinkedIn, a company can share information,
promote events, research their customers' needs, and even get a better
understanding of their competition. And LinkedIn company pages are
not only used by for-profit corporations, but by entities such as nonprofits and political candidates as well.

LinkedIn also has some interesting tools and new features. Content
Marketing Score is a new feature, introduced in 2014, which measures
the reach and engagement of your pages, groups, and updates. You
receive a score which you can compare against your competition, as well
as recommendations on how to improve. This is a great way to track the
success of your social media strategy.

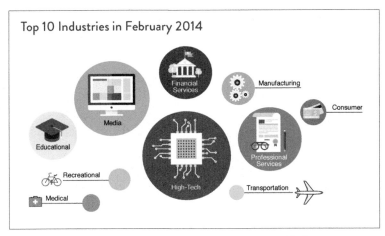

Top 10 Industries in 2014 based on average Content Marketing Score on LinkedIn.

Trending Content is a tool that measures which issues have gotten the most engagement with specific audiences; it's a helpful tool to monitor trends, breaking news, and current themes, and can help you tailor your content for greater relevance.

Most trending topics on LinkedIn. *Source:* www.linkedin.com[73]

LinkedIn Today, now renamed "Pulse," is a news product launched in 2011. It allows you to see the articles and stories that are being read most by your contacts and people in your industry, helping you stay up-to-date with current developments pertaining to your business.

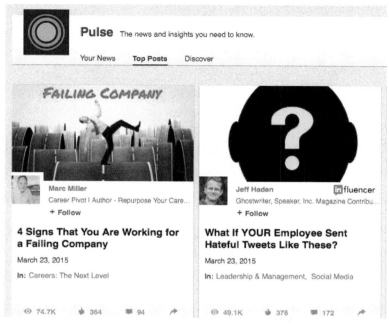

LinkedIn Today is also known as Pulse. This screenshot shows the top posts for the day on February 25. *Source:* www.linkedin.com[74]

Showcase Pages is a tool launched in 2013; a showcase page enables you to highlight a specific product, service, assignment, or department. These pages can be followed by users, so it's a good idea to update them periodically with new developments and fresh material.

As in every other social media network, you should also focus on providing interesting and valuable updates which may help others succeed in business; especially popular are posts sharing industry insights, expertise, and company developments. Ask questions or ask for feedback to increase engagement, and use compelling photos or images. You'll need to consistently post valuable material; a rate of about one or two updates a day is probably ideal. Keep up-to-date with comments from your network, and respond promptly.

ACTION STEPS FOR LINKEDIN

1. Optimize your personal profile by making sure you have relevant keywords in your heading and profile.

2. Make sure your profile URL is easy to guess and enter into a browser's address bar. You may need to edit it to remove the numbers that may have been assigned to it when you created your LinkedIn account.

3. Start connecting with people you have worked with, and make sure you get a few recommendations and endorsement.

4. Post updates on LinkedIn about work-related successes and/or industry news a few times a week.

5. Be creative: See if you can connect with people in real life by making connections on LinkedIn. See chapter 12 for Peter Kuperman's story.

6. Set up your company page and get your employees to start joining it.

7. Showcase important news and job opportunities on your company page.

8. Always be professional and polite.

9. Connect with people you know, and politely decline people you don't know. Your network is most valuable if you really know all the people in it.

13.6 YOUTUBE

Today, YouTube is the world's most popular site for viewing and sharing videos online. With the current generation of smartphones, almost everyone has the ability to easily create, upload, and share videos with the world, and videos can easily be watched on-the-go or shared with friends. YouTube has also become the world's second largest search engine: People actively turn to YouTube to search for information and find out about things that they want to know, aside from using it for entertainment purposes. Here are some tips to help you get the most out of YouTube and video content more generally.

Start by setting up your YouTube Channel. Choose a good username that represents your brand or company without being too cumbersome.

You may want to choose a name that is consistent with your Google+ account or business page, as that will make things easier to manage; you should also link your website with your YouTube channel. As with all other social media profiles, fill out your profile and "about" section completely, with updated information and keywords that accurately describe your content. Upload a clear and recognizable profile photo, as well as banner art representative of your channel. Make sure your channel cover is big enough to look good on a big screen TV, as many people are now viewing YouTube on TV. See https://support.google.com/youtube/answer/2972003?hl=en for instructions for adding your channel art, and follow the dimension recommendations below.

Dimensions for your YouTube Channel Art (cover or main image). *Source:* www.google.com[75]

You can also create a trailer for a YouTube channel, which can be seen by viewers who are not already subscribers; this trailer can help potential fans learn what your channel is all about, so make it short and convincing! Similarly, YouTube has a Fan Finder feature which will show a brief video to viewers who might be interested in your channel. These videos must be two minutes or less; if you don't have time to create one, you could always use your trailer. Within your channel, you can create playlists and groups to highlight specific content.

As far as quality goes, YouTube viewers generally do not expect professional actors, and they also do not expect professional, Hollywood-level production values. In many cases, videos will be quite short (often

5 minutes or less), and can even have been shot on a smart phone or flip camera. Obviously, a video that looks and sounds terrible will reflect poorly on your business, so you should take care that there is adequate lighting, that the chosen camera angles show things clearly, and that the picture is not too shaky. If you plan on using videos pretty extensively, you may want to invest in some basic editing equipment, lighting, or microphones; for many companies, however, that won't be necessary.

In most cases, it is really the content more than the production value that matters most. Just about anything that you could produce in a written format could be done by video—for example, sharing news, making announcements, discussing opinions, press releases, tutorials, and so on. James Wedmore offers an extensive series of YouTube tutorials, so look him up on YouTube for your very own free YouTube University series.

For your videos, you may want to interview experts or record product demos. The Will It Blend series is a great introduction to this concept. You could create a series with multiple videos and encourage people to watch each new episode; you could also ask and answer questions with your audience. But it's important to hook viewers with something catchy or intriguing right from the beginning of your video: If things are moving too slowly, people are likely to turn it off or switch to another channel, so avoid lengthy titles and boring introductions. Of course, some types of videos may run longer than a few minutes, depending on the topic and material—but in every case try to keep it enjoyable and entertaining as much as possible, and make sure it doesn't feel like a marketing pitch!

Try to find a cheery, likeable person to feature in your videos, someone who will appeal to your audience and can speak naturally—not like a scripted robot. Ideas for videos include interviewing experts, introducing viewers to members of your staff, or showing a motivational speech made by one of your executives. You may also want to feature a call to action in some of your videos, asking viewers to like the particular video or subscribe to your channel.

Another technique is to use annotations, which are clickable text overlays that appear on the video, somewhat like captions: You can use annotations to provide additional information, or to highlight information that you forgot or for some other reason could not include when you filmed the video. Using annotations is also a convenient way to reuse an old video by adding new information or updates onto it. Finally, you can use annotations to ask for likes, comments, and subscriptions, or to provide links or other contact information. Annotations are quite customizable; you can choose the color, type, size, duration, and number of annotations that appear, but it's a good idea not to go overboard with them—you don't want to detract from the picture or make your video impossible to watch. On YouTube it is also possible to add a company watermark to your videos, which will highlight your brand name.

Although we have mainly discussed YouTube here, videos can be shared across most of the social media platforms, so don't forget to leverage your reach by providing links and "like" and "share" buttons. You can optimize your YouTube strategy by writing effective descriptions and titles, tagging your video with appropriate keywords, and captioning it or providing a transcript. And just like in other forms of social media, you need to be posting consistently, and to be responsive to comments, complaints, and questions from your audience. Whenever possible, make it interactive by inviting your audience to share their own videos, or by running a special contest or event.

ACTION STEPS FOR YOUTUBE

1. Get a good camera. Actually, your iPhone should be fine, but make sure the sound quality of your video is good.

2. Watch a few how-to videos and/or videos that are similar to the kind of video you are planning to make in order to get some tips for how to shoot, what works and what doesn't, etc.

3. Build your YouTube channel, adding channel art and a profile picture. Note that your YouTube account and activity is usually connected to Google+.

4. Make sure that you are tagging, annotating, and using good keywords in the title of your video in order for it to be easily found when people search. Remember that YouTube is the second largest search engine.

5. Once you have uploaded a video, remember to share it on all your other social networks.

6. If you're wondering how to make your video go viral, you may want to think about the following, as recommended in "Five Reasons the KONY Video Went Viral:" [76]

   a) Tell a story.
   b) Make the video about them, your audience, not you.
   c) Make the video action-packed.
   d) Get celebrities or top influencers to share the video.
   e) Include a "To Be Continued..." or plan a series.

13.7 INSTAGRAM

The free photo-sharing app Instagram was launched in 2010 and was originally available only on smartphones (iPhone and Android). It has grown to 300 million users, including everyone from casual shutterbugs to avid photographers. On Instagram, users take a photo (or a video), apply a filter and add a caption if they so wish, and share it on Instagram or other social media. Instagram users connect with their friends, or follow interesting people and companies. Users "like" photos and can leave comments for the photographer. The @ symbol is used to tag specific users, and the hashtag # is used—just like on Twitter—to create categories. There is also a direct messaging system so users can share a photo privately with another user, without posting it to all of their followers.

Get started by completing your profile in full, adding details about your company and appropriate links, and choosing a profile picture that fits the circle used on Instagram profiles. Find and invite your friends. Attract followers by linking your Instagram profile to your other social media platforms and offering special promotions to your Instagram followers. Share your Instagram on other social media platforms such as Facebook. It's a good idea to use the Explore tab where you can browse photos to get a feel for the culture of Instagram, check out some of the trends, and get inspired.

On Instagram, there is definitely a preference for artistic, well-done photos; in other words, quality over quantity. It's a good idea to pick your one best photo to share, rather than posting ten mediocre images. Many brands on Instagram post once a day or less, not multiple times per day as you might do on Twitter, for example.

There are some general tips for creating quality photos that apply to old-fashioned film cameras as well as Instagram. First and foremost, Instagram photos are shown as squares, so you should imagine your composition as a square (not a rectangle like older cameras). Fortunately, most smart phone cameras have a square mode, so that's easy to do. Composition is important; the "rule of thirds" can help you create a great image. Imagine that your view is divided into thirds, either horizontally or vertically, and then balance your composition accordingly. Another composition tip is to experiment with symmetry, which produces great results in Instagram's square format. Experiment with different camera angles, for example shooting from a higher or lower position, from one side, or from behind your subject. Playing with the zoom and focus controls can produce interesting results; close-up photos can be especially nice for showing product details.

After you've taken the photo, there are a number of editing and technical details to consider. Will you be branding your photo? (For a more detailed discussion of branding images, see section 8.4). If so, apply the frames, filters, colors, or captions that correspond to your brand. A variety of filters are available, and can be quite fun to use. However, there is generally a preference for photos that are not edited and filtered to the point of obscuring reality. And if you have a naturally stunning photo, you might not even want to use a filter; see the #nofilter hashtag for examples. Remember that you don't have to take the original photo in the Instagram app. It is possible to import photos that you shot with your mobile's camera, and this can be useful if your mobile device has editing tools that are not available on Instagram.

Paid advertising on Instagram will be rolling out in early 2015; unless you are a paid advertiser, you are not obligated to follow these guidelines, but they are useful as good indicators of the type of material that is preferred. In brief, they discourage overly heavy use of filters that mask the reality of the photo. Text overlays are not allowed, and brands cannot feature their logo in the shot unless it is an unobtrusive part of the scene. Ads should be "true to your brand," which means not shocking or gimmicky. Photos are encouraged to capture "moments" rather than products—in other words, you should offer something more creative than just an image of an item. Ads are also asked to "take cues" from the existing Instagram community, and especially to make use of popular hashtags. That means you should respect the general "vibe" of Instagram and not post things that are wildly out of place. Remember that Instagram is owned by Facebook, so the advertising rules and tools are likely to be similar to Facebook's.

There are a lot of options for promoting yourself via this platform. You can use the caption space to describe a product, ask a question, or provide links or other information; similarly, you can use hashtags to categorize your content and make it easy for users to find. For example, one local record shop posts photos of its new arrivals, hashtagging the names of the bands, and in the caption they list prices and store hours, thereby encouraging local customers to come in to the store if they see something they want to buy. Taking that idea a step further, you can advertise special offers, promotions, or flash sales to your Instagram fans. Many businesses post something along the lines of "Mention this ad for 10% off today." Instagram contests are also quite popular; you just need to choose a prize, figure out an entry method, then publicize your contest to your fans, monitor the progress, and announce a winner. You can also use the "like" feature, promising to reveal a surprise or special offer if your photo gets enough likes. You can "re-gram" or repost other users' photos, crediting them accordingly, of course. And you can use Instagram's geo-tagging feature, which allows you to tag photos with the location where they were taken and then add that information to a Photo Map. One last way to reach out to your followers is to leave meaningful comments—a thank you or a friendly message—on their photos as well.

With so much going on, you may want to schedule the delivery of your posts in order to maximize the impact of campaigns and promotions. However, at this time Instagram does not have a built-in scheduling function, so you will have to use a third-party app (for example, Latergramme) which allows you to queue content and choose posting times. Another way to manage your content is by using Instagram Direct, which allows you to share private messages or group messages with up to fifteen people. You can use the private message feature to deal with disputes privately, rather than in the public comments section. And you could identify your most dedicated fans and then send them promotions or special offers via the group feature. Automation tools are generally discouraged in order to keep communications real and organic, but you may want to look at Instagress if you need to be more active on Instagram but don't have the time to be looking at every photo posted about your niche.

Aside from photography, it's possible to film and post videos on Instagram. (For more extensive tips on videos, see chapter 8.5.) On Instagram, the video length must be a minimum of three and maximum of fifteen seconds. Similar to the photo function, you can shoot video "in app," or you can import video from your phone's camera roll. Instagram's editing features are fairly basic, and you'll probably have more tools and editing capabilities at your disposal if you use the second option. If you're concerned about creating a quality video that you can also use for other purposes, then importing is probably the way to go. Instagram has a pretty good video mode called "Cinema," which removes wobble and gives your video a steady, professional feel; but if you're also going to be using the video on another platform such as Facebook or YouTube, you'll be well advised to shoot it outside of Instagram. Another cool feature to experiment with is the Hyperlapse app, which allows you to shoot time-lapse videos on your mobile device. (This is not a feature in Instagram itself, but an independent app launched by Instagram.) Although it sounds short, 15 seconds can actually feel like a long time to be watching something, especially if it's an ad. So if you're using Instagram videos to promote something, you should probably keep it short. To entice viewers, choose an attractive cover frame; this is what your viewers will see in their feeds as well as in search results.

ACTION STEPS FOR INSTAGRAM

1. Download the Instagram app and/or create an account at www.instagram.com.

2. Scroll through the "discover" screen to see what kinds of images other people are posting. You can also look up a competitor brand on Instagram on the web, by browsing to http://www.Instagram.com /CompetitorName (where "CompetitorName" is obviously the name of your competitor).

3. Take a few photos and play with the filters so that you understand how they work and you can find and refine your style.

4. Start following people on Instagram that the app suggests; they will pop up based on your Facebook network.

5. If you're using the account for a business, be sure to set up your editorial calendar and build an image vault or lineup that will allow you to post according to your schedule.

6. You may also want to consider running a few contests on Instagram by asking people to tag images with your brand name or a specific hashtag in order to build content around a specific topic.

PIER 39's Instagram account as viewed on the web at https://instagram.com/pier39/.
Source: www.instagram.com[77]

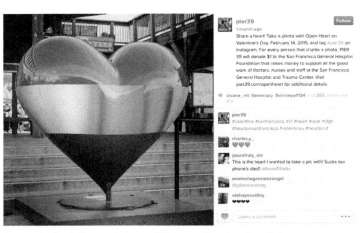

An example of a challenge on Instagram. This is a good way to get people to engage with your brand on Instagram. *Source:* www.instagram.com[78]

13.8 VINE

Vine is an app developed in 2013 that allows users to record six-second video clips, which then play in an endless loop. Similar to other social media platforms, there are many creative ways for brands to share content on Vine without being overly self-promotional.

The first tip is to be inventive and humorous. It's a good idea to check out some of the funny video themes that have become popular trends on Vine; you can easily find "best of" collections on YouTube. Funny kids, cute animals, parodies of popular culture, and everyday occurrences are always popular and hilarious topics. Secondly, be helpful. Just like on other social media platforms, you can share tips, tricks, how-tos and instructions with your followers. While it may sound impossible to create a tutorial in just six seconds, Lowe's hardware store did a great job with their "Five in Six" campaign, which did exactly that. Third, collaborate with popular Vine users, related businesses or peers, or influential people. You could appear in their videos and vice versa. Fourth, share your customers' stories. Encourage customers to share videos featuring your products, mentioning your username and appropriate hashtag so you can find and repost them to your own Vine feed easily. And fifth, encourage sharing by posting your Vine clips on other sites such as Twitter, Facebook, and Instagram.

Technical considerations for producing a good quality Vine video are much the same as for other photo and video projects, but with some specific challenges due to the six-second format. It's usually a good idea to think through what you want to record before you get started; try to plan out how you want it to look and what camera angles and composition will work best; this is called a storyboard in film and video, and works well for Vine too. Initially, recording with Vine was done in one take, which made planning it out even more essential. However, Vine now provides a Sessions mode, which allows you to save a recording and work on it later, even removing and reorganizing shots before you share your video. In Vine, tapping or pressing the screen will start a recording, so you could press and hold to create a single, continuous six-second shot. Alternatively, by pressing, releasing, and pressing again repeatedly you can create a kind of stop-motion animation. Some highly-practiced

Vine users can get 140 taps into a single video, thus creating 24 frames per second as in real movies. Finally, as in every other photo and video project, keep in mind lighting, focus, and camera stillness in order to produce the best images.

There are a number of techniques you can use to really make your Vine content stand out. Vine videos now appear in the newsfeed with a "cover photo," which is actually the top half of the first frame of the Vine video. If you plan ahead, you can choose an attractive or intriguing first frame, so that when users scroll through and see the cover photo they will become interested in actually watching the video. As detailed in the previous paragraph, you could consider making a stop-motion animation video. Alternatively, since Vine videos automatically replay themselves, you could plan your video so that it is a seamless loop of action: Instead of a scene that abruptly ends at six seconds and then repeats, try to film an action that transitions naturally from end to beginning over and over again. Get experimental, like a real filmmaker; try sound-only videos with a minimal background image, or 360-degree videos which are great for showing off scenery, buildings, or other interesting locations. Use different camera techniques such as panning or placing your camera on a makeshift dolly to move it along. Last but not least, get creative with your storytelling. You'd be surprised at how much narrative and action you can pack into just six seconds. For some of the best Vine examples, look for Zach King on YouTube or Vine—he is someone who has truly mastered the art of the Vine.

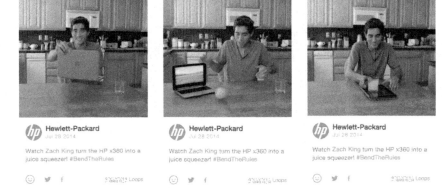

Three frames from a Vine video made by Vine expert Zach King. *Source:* www.youtube.com[79]

ACTION STEPS FOR VINE

1. Download the Vine app.

2. See https://vine.co/ for vine examples, or search for Zach King on YouTube.

3. As with all social media, it's a good idea to experiment with the tool before posting anything publicly. Play with the Vine app so that you can see how the looping works.

4. Storyboard out your idea for a Vine, and make sure the looping will be smooth.

5. Once you have developed an excellent Vine video, share it on your other social networks, starting with Twitter.

13.9 SNAPCHAT

Launched in 2011, Snapchat is a relatively new entity in the social media field but it has nevertheless become enormously popular, gaining more than 100 million active monthly users by 2015. Snapchat is a photo and video sharing service, but what makes it unique is that the message permanently self-destructs within one to ten seconds of being viewed by the recipient. The sender specifies the time limit, and can also modify a photo or video with filters, captions, and text. Snapchat's users are primarily teens and young adults. Because of Snapchat's ephemeral nature, it's really well-suited to humor, one-of-a-kind or in-the-moment images, sharing secrets, or exchanging tiny conversations. There's a sense of excitement and anticipation about seeing what kind of "snap" you'll receive, and you have to really pay attention as you won't be able to see the photo or message again.

There are a number of ways Snapchat can be used for effective marketing. You could ask your customers a simple question or make a request— for example "Snap a photo when you're wearing our shoes!"—but keep in mind that text time and space is limited, so you'll need to be concise. You can be humorous by using Snapchat's editing features to add funny faces, doodles, or emoticons to your images; this will help keep followers interested. Snapchat is an ideal platform for sharing sneak peeks, previews, and exclusive content, and if need be, you can spread content out over the course of several snaps in a series. You can also use Snapchat to send out coupons or special offers—but again, remember that because your audience can't "keep" the message, it'll have to be short and clear.

Try creating a Snapchat contest, quiz, or game for your followers. Make a quiz or puzzle by sending clues over a period of time; in the end, your followers can win a prize by "solving" the quiz. Or send out a snap requesting something specific, and the first follower to snap back wins a prize.

A new feature on Snapchat is the "Stories" mode, which allows you to join multiple snaps together, creating a continuing reel of snaps. The oldest snaps will be deleted after 24 hours, and to keep the story going you'll need to add new content regularly. You can use this feature to create an extended narrative; another benefit is that in Snapchat Stories, the snap is not deleted after 10 seconds, so this gives your audience an extended viewing time. Whether you're in regular Snapchat or Stories mode, you have to take your photos and videos within the app; it is not possible to import photos or videos from another source, and this can make pre-planning a bit tricky and more important than on other platforms.

You can increase your Snapchat following by asking existing followers to recommend you to their friends; you may want to send a reward (like a discount code) after they do so, and send out welcome messages and/or special offers to your new fans. Snapchat (unlike Facebook or Instagram) does not provide analytic tools to businesses, so if you want to track your activity or followers you'll have to do it manually. Finally, combine Snapchat with your other social media platforms, for example by letting your Twitter or Facebook followers know about a contest that you're running on Snapchat.

Did you know that some big brands are already trying to connect with users on Snapchat? Snapchat's Discover is flipping the dominant paradigm in that it is now offering advertisers full control over what they show on the platform. Instead of the norm of the social platform showing what's popular based on user interactions, Snapchat is allowing editorial teams to select what news they provide; and judging from the launch video, this feature looks very slick.

ACTION STEPS FOR SNAPCHAT

1. Download the app.

2. Invite a few of your friends to start snapping with you.

3. Understand the platform before trying to connect with the audience

4. Understand what the audience is expecting on Snapchat.

5. Develop a Snapchat campaign that is fun and rewarding for Snapchat users. They are likely to be young, with very short attention spans, so fast and funny is the way to go with Snapchat.

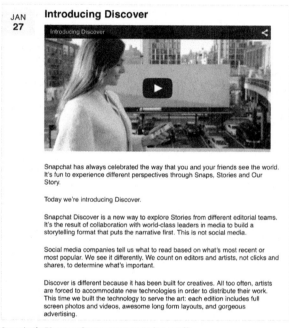

Snapchat's Discover. *Source:* www.snapchat.com[80]

In a world where people have increasingly shorter attention spans and an ever-growing need for stimulation, along with the expectation of not only being treated respectfully but even being wooed by competing companies, to survive as a business you'll need to not only understand your audience as if it were to become your spouse; you'll also need to develop a deep understanding of each and every social media platform.

ENDNOTES

1 www.conversationprism.com

2 www.sprinklr.com/resources/whitepapers/social-media-dream-team/

3 www.chocolateforbreakfast.com

4 https://www.facebook.com/chocolateforbreakfast/photos/a.158370317532877
.25109.152143361488906/790411570995412/?type=1&theater

5 http://www.shutterstock.com/cat.mhtml?searchterm=SMART%20
goal&language=en&lang=en&search_source=&safesearch=1&version
=llv1&media_type=&media_type2=images&search_cat=&searchtermx
=&photographer_name=&people_gender=&people_age=&people_ethnicity
=&people_number=&color=&page=1&inline=30041584

6 https://twitter.com/search?f=realtime&q=%23welcomeHome%20%40
ckmarie23&src=typd

7 http://mashable.com/2011/02/16/red-cross-tweet/

8 http://mashable.com/2011/02/16/red-cross-tweet/

9 http://mashable.com/2011/02/16/red-cross-tweet/

10 https://twitter.com/hiltonsuggests

11 http://blogs.imediaconnection.com/blog/2013/02/06/lessons-in-real-time
-media-sb47/

12 https://www.facebook.com/Discovery

13 www.facebook.com/pier39

14 https://www.facebook.com/ads/create/?campaign_id=276899725739312
&placement=tcr&extra_1=is-admgr-user

15 https://www.youtube.com/watch?v=SGoVVrqe2t8

16 http://www.facebook.com/Bissell

17 http://www.facebook.com/Bissell

18 http://likealyzer.com/bissell

19 https://www.youtube.com/watch?v=jottDMuLesU

20 https://twitter.com/jkrums/status/1121915133

21 http://www.twitpic.com/135xa

22 https://www.facebook.com/pages/create/

23 http://www.facebook.com

24 http://www.facebook.com

25 http://www.facebook.com

26 https://www.facebook.com/ads/create

27 http://blog.wishpond.com/post/108543514327/should-your-business
    -say-goodbye-to-facebook

28 http://www.linkedin.com

29 https://www.linkedin.com/company/adobe

30 https://www.pinterest.com/search/
    pins/?q=surfing&term_meta%5B%5D=surfing%7Ctyped

31 https://www.pinterest.com/pin/235031674279703837/

32 http://www.pinterest.com/chobani

33 http://www.pinterest.com/chobani

34 http://www.digitalinformationworld.com/2015/02/fascinating-social
    -networking-stats-2015.html

35 http://www.alsa.org/fight-als/ice-bucket-challenge.html

36 http://www.alsa.org/fight-als/ice-bucket-challenge.html

37 http://cdn1.sharpspring.com/companies/M7QwMwMA/uploads/eBooks
    /persona_template.pdf

38 http://www.facebook.com/KingOscarSeafood

39 http://www.facebook.com/KingOscarSeafood

40 http://www.facebook.com/KingOscarSeafood

41 https://www.youtube.com/watch?v=ZUG9qYTJMsI

42 https://www.youtube.com/watch?v=OhBmWxQpedI&feature=youtu.be

43 https://www.youtube.com/watch?v=dem6eA7-A2I&feature=youtu.be

44 http://www.kaushik.net/avinash/web-analytics-success-
    measurement-government-websites/

45 http://dailycrowdsource.com/daily-crowdsourcing-files/images
    -crowdsourcing/article-images/daily-article-images/2014/11
    /revolution-tools-610x454.jpg

46 https://www.threadless.com/make/submit/

47 http://dailycrowdsource.com/content/crowdsourcing/1420-what-happens
    -when-crowdsourcing-and-social-media-merge

48 http://www.facebook.com/Cisco

49 https://twitter.com/Charmin/status/566627940843401216

50 http://www.facebook.com/Cisco

51 https://www.facebook.com/backunmusical and https://www.facebook.com
    /search/str/%2312DaysOfBackun/keywords_top

52 https://www.facebook.com/backunmusical and https://www.facebook.com
    /search/str/%2312DaysOfBackun/keywords_top

53 http://memegenerator.net/instance/59426378

54 http://www.wired.com/2013/02/oreo-twitter-super-bowl/

55 http://youtube/CHtyQJzTy70

56 https://twitter.com/searls/status/573614339132796928

57 https://twitter.com/united/status/572551694032232448

58 https://rlstollar.wordpress.com/2013/02/02/applebees-overnight-social
    -media-meltdown-a-photo-essay

59 https://twitter.com/CVS_Extra/status/570652124742332418

60 https://www.youtube.com/watch?v=dem6eA7-A2I&feature=youtu.be

61 https://www.facebook.com/media/set/?set=a.402599190676.183521
    .26483215676

62 Kerpen, D. (2011). Likeable Social Media: How to Delight Your Customers,
    Create and Irresistable Brand and Be Generally Amazing on Facebook (and
    Other Social Networks). McGraw Hill.

63 http://mashable.com/2015/02/25/live-moon/

64 http://www.peterkuperman.com

65 http://www.digitalinformationworld.com/2015/02/fascinating-social
-networking-stats-2015.html

66 https://www.facebook.com/target

67 http://www.twitter.com/susby

68 http://www.twitter.com/

69 https://plus.google.com/u/0/s/ripples?cfem=1

70 RJMetrics https://blog.rjmetrics.com/2014/05/07/pinners-be-pinnin
-how-to-justify-pinterests-3-8b-valuation/

71 https://www.youtube.com/watch?v=e5FM-VcE7UA

72 https://www.youtube.com/watch?v=e5FM-VcE7UA

73 https://business.linkedin.com/marketing-solutions/c/14/3/content
-marketing-score

74 https://www.linkedin.com/today/posts

75 https://support.google.com/youtube/answer/2972003?hl=en

76 http://www.businessweek.com/articles/2012-03-16/five-reasons-the
-kony-video-went-viral#p1

77 https://instagram.com/pier39/

78 https://instagram.com/p/zDbK36g3uk/?modal=true

79 https://www.youtube.com/watch?v=nIve4LVLDJk

80 http://blog.snapchat.com/post/109302961090/introducing-discover

INDEX

CPSIA information can be obtained at www.ICGtesting.com
Printed in the USA
LVOW05s2320160615

442760LV00044B/827/P

9 781623 155728